Kentucky Wild:
The Films of William Girdler

By Ian Cooper

BearManor Media.com

Typesetting and layout by PKJ Passion Global

Published in the USA by
BearManor Media
1317 Edgewater Dr #110
Orlando FL 32804
www.BearManorMedia.com

Softcover Edition
ISBN-10:
ISBN-13: 979-8-88771-415-8

Published in the USA by Bear Manor Media

Table of Contents

Acknowledgements

I´m very grateful to a number of people, without whom this book wouldn´t exist in the form it does but primarily, I´m indebted to Ben Ohmart. Without his support and encouragement the book wouldn´t exist at all. I also owe a considerable debt to the late Patricia ´Patty´ Breen, whose website *WilliamGirdler.com* is still the definitive web resource for anyone interested in his films. A number of Girdler´s collaborators were nice enough to give me their time and assistance. David Sheldon, Andrew Stevens and Graham Masterton answered all of my questions and offered some illuminating and often very funny anecdotes. I´m especially grateful to Don Wrege, who not only provided insight into the making of *Asylum of Satan* but also was kind enough to let me use some of his photographs from the shoot. Thomas Pope not only shared his experiences of working with Bill but also provided me with a copy of his screenplay for *The Manitou* and treatments for a number of unmade Girdler/Pope collaborations. Unless stated otherwise, all of the quotes from Sheldon, Stevens, Masterton, Wrege and Pope come from their various conversations with me that took place throughout 2021.

Introduction

I've been a fan of William Girdler for almost as long as I can remember. In 1977, my tenth birthday present was a family outing to the Odeon Cinema in Crewe to see *Grizzly*. I loved it and thought it was the best thing since *Jaws* (and even at that tender age I realized that Girdler's film owed a considerable debt to Spielberg). The 70s was another country and they certificated films differently there, so despite it being cut for an A certificate a considerable amount of blood and savagery remained. It was too much for my mother and it was the last time we went to the cinema as a family. Decades later, I attempted to pass the torch to my eight-year-old son and showed him the film on DVD, although he bailed after a few minutes when a severed arm flew through the air. We took refuge in another Girdler, the arguably bleaker but less graphic *Day of the Animals* and he ended up both thrilled and annoyed by the (very 70s) ambiguous ending which hints at the horrors that lay in wait for us unless we clean up our environmental act. Towards the end of 2020, I was watching *Three on a Meathook* for the first time and on a late-night whim after a couple of glasses of red wine, I pitched a book about Girdler to Ben at Bear Manor. He replied positively a couple of hours later and before the week was out, I'd signed a contract to write the book you're reading. There's something very fitting about a book on exploitation film going from initial conception to green light in such a short time.

Chapter 1 - Girdler, Kentucky and the Art of the Rip-Off

If you really stop to think about it, life on both a small and large scale makes very little rational sense. No, we rarely find ourselves floating naked in space trading laser blasts out of our hands with a malevolent deformed midget, but that's beside the point. Look at any life; any historical event with cold reason, and it rarely makes any logical sense. Stuff just happens, some of it pretty damned weird and inexplicable. It's just the way things work sometimes (Knipfel 2017).

William Girdler's career was short, lasting just six years but even by the standards of those who toil away in the exploitation arena, he was extremely prolific, making nine features between 1972 and 1978, when he was killed in a helicopter crash in the jungle outside Manila, aged only thirty. He's never been anything other than a marginal figure and is largely known today for *The Manitou* although a number of his other features have their devoted followers, in no small part due to his working in the kind of fields – horror, science fiction, Blaxploitation – that appeal to the rabid film fan. Some of his films made a lot of money, especially *Grizzly*, which held the title of most successful independent film until deposed by *Halloween* (1978) but he was critically maligned during his lifetime and little has changed in the intervening decades. Indeed, most writing about Girdler emphasizes both his status as youthful prodigy and that critical disdain:

To this day he's relatively unknown, generally under-appreciated by the late-night TV horror crowd, and yet persists as an underground, underdog hero, especially in the state from which he hailed, Kentucky (Harris 2020).

Though largely ignored by mainstream film buffs, and sorely underappreciated by trash genre devotees, William Girdler Sr.

remains one of Hollywood history's most prolific directors (Breen 2000-1).

Director William Girdler (1947-78 helicopter crash) made only nine features in his career which spanned the 1970s. Most are considered rubbish by the critics. But when you look at what Girdler did with so little money, you can't be anything but impressed (cultfilmalley 2020).

Unsurprisingly, Girdler was a movie nut and his filmography features some eclectic casts made up of minor Louisville celebrities, well-known cult actors and a handful of faded stars of yesteryear who found themselves adrift in the exploitation field. Off-screen too, he mixed with a motley collection of colorful characters, from the many family members he pressed into service to ufologists, a shady producer who disappeared, a spook show performer turned fake gore provider, a handful of horror hosts and a veteran screenwriter who ended up being jailed after running guns for the Irish National Liberation Army. Girdler's habitat, that netherworld of low-budget, regionally-made exploitation has much in common with the early years of cinema when film-making was almost exclusively, to quote Werner Herzog, "not the art of scholars but of illiterates" (Herzog in Kent 1977:83), sideshow performers, hucksters and assorted misfits. Take Tod Browning, another horror director from Louisville born nearly 70 years before Girdler, who worked as a carnival barker, blackface performer, song and dance man and "Living Hypnotic Corpse" before turning to directing films via stints as an actor and screenwriter.

As much as in the more prestigious arena of arthouse film, authorship is greatly prized among exploitation fans with directors like Russ Meyer, Jesus/Jess Franco or Lucio Fulci being lionized in much the same way as Fellini, Pasolini or Bunuel are feted by conventional cineastes. While directors including Wes Craven and David Cronenberg achieved something like critical respectability and the higher profiles and budgets that come with that, even the most marginal of exploitation auteurs can eventually end up celebrated and rediscovered by new audiences. In recent years, directors such as Al Adamson and William Griefe have been the subject of lavish Blu-Ray box-sets and critical reassessment. The most striking turnaround has been the case of Andy Milligan, the director of a string of misanthropic, oddly personal genre films with eye-catching title such as *The Bloodthirsty Butchers* (1970) and *The Rats are Coming, The Werewolves are Here* (1972). In his lifetime he was widely regarded as a bottom of the barrel hack, a position best summed up by Michael J. Weldon's suggestion that "If you're an Andy Milligan fan there's no hope for you" (Weldon 1983:273) and after his AIDS-related death in 1991, he was buried in a pauper's grave. But the intervening years have seen a comprehensive Milligan biography (*The Ghastly One* by Jimmy McDonough [2001]), a box-set of 14 films packed with special features and a couple of his features released by the British Film Institute. Such plaudits have so far escaped William Girdler but surely it's only a matter of time.

Girdler specialized in low-budget reworkings of popular films and like the Italian exploitation directors who churned out endless variations on the films of the Georges Romero and Miller, he's held in great affection, if never really generating the kind of extravagant praise dished out to the more innovative genre directors. He's been described variously as "King of the Knockoffs" (Knipfel 2016) and "a man who made a mess of lovely movies that rode the tails of other movies" (Alexander 2016), cast as the high priest of a "rip-off cult" (cultfilmalley 2020) and even been somewhat uncharitably dubbed "Kentucky's Ed Wood" (Harris 2020). The director himself was open about his motivations, "Hitchcock is my idol. He's great; he's the only director whose pictures people will go see just off his name alone - because they know they'll be entertained" (Girdler in Breen 2000-1).

The director's adoration for Hitchcock, someone who was able to make highly personal and very profitable films within the Hollywood system is revealing. Unlike many other young directors who worship the rebellious outsiders like Welles and Cassavetes or any number of European auteurs, Girdler always aspired to make popular cinema. He explained his approach to Graham Masterton, author of the source novel for *The Manitou*, "My aim is to make the audience laugh one minute so that they're relaxed and the next minute to scare the shit out of them." This desire to give the paying audience an experience comes up time and again in interviews with the director. In an obituary, his hometown paper, *The Louisville Courier-Journal* quoted Girdler talking about the kind of acclaim that eluded him, good notices and prestigious awards:

All I want to do is to entertain people and make a profit for my investors. If I do win one (an Academy Award) and start getting good reviews, that'll be fine too. But the approval that means the most right now is the approval the public give me when they pay $30 million to see one of my pictures. Their approval is what counts (anon. a 1978).

The Art of the Rip-Off or Ripping-Off Art

When I was first called a (rip-off artist), I got really offended. But everybody who makes a film is a rip-off artist. Ripping off an audience is a much more serious thing than ripping off a story. (Girdler in Breen 2000-1)

Jean-Luc Godard proposed some years ago that the only adequate way to review one film is to make another in response. A director named William Girdler apparently agrees. He's on his way to the creation of an entire oeuvre of such movies (Canby 1976).

There's a thin line between paying homage and ripping off with even the most innovative cinematic landmarks in debt to their predecessors. Janet Leigh was terrorized in a motel in *Touch of Evil* (1958) before she met Mrs. Bates in *Psycho* (1960) and *Night of the Living Dead* (1968) may well never have been made if Richard Matheson hadn't written *I am Legend* (1954). At best, Girdler is Prince of the Knockoffs, with the undisputed King being Roger Corman. Corman's lengthy career as producer, director and uniquely gifted talent-spotter makes it abundantly clear that you can turn the rip-off into art. A cultured man and talented director who enthusiastically took on the mantle of exploitation huckster, Corman is a key figure in American cinema. As well as giving the likes of Scorsese, Coppola, Bogdanovich, Hopper, Nicholson and countless others their first breaks in what amounted to an informal film school, his unique sensibility – churning out cheap genre movies, gangster, science fiction and horror films, creature features, acid and biker exposes while also distributing Bergman and Fellini – was a major influence on the Hollywood New Wave. *The Godfather* (1972), *The Exorcist* (1974) and *Taxi Driver* (1976) all feature semi-exploitation plots married to European arthouse style while *Jaws* (1975), directed by a 26-year-old *wunderkind* is exactly the kind of film AIP could've turned out if they were willing to come up with that kind of budget. Corman made his name with a string of Poe adaptations that borrowed liberally from Hammer and Italian genre directors and were elevated by a talented cast and crew, be it writers such as Robert Towne, Richard Matheson and Charles Beaumont or veteran actors such as Boris Karloff, Peter Lorre and Basil Rathbone. Vincent Price, the star of many of the entries, had also been around for a long time and was 50 when he made the first in the series, *House of Usher* (1969) but his very striking performances, seeming both creepy and at the same time in on the joke, proved invaluable (when Ray Milland replaced Price in *The Premature Burial* [1962] the film was considerably less effective). Despite his claims to the contrary, it's hard to believe Corman when he says that he didn't intend to shamelessly lift from *The Seventh Seal* (1957) for *Masque of the Red Death* (1964) (see Biodrowski 2007) while as both producer and director he oversaw numerous variations on the Depression-era gangster hit, *Bonnie and Clyde* (1967). There were also a number of *zeitgeisty* ripped-from-the-headlines items like *The Wild Angels* (1968) and *The Trip* (1968), which enthusiastically exploited the counterculture, whether it be motorcycles gangs or acidheads. After departing AIP in 1970, he set up New World Pictures with brother Gene and along with a lot of women-in-prison, sexy nurse, biker and

Blaxploitation films, the company would go on to oversee some striking and witty take-offs of big studio hits which, true to form, gave breaks to some unsung talents. *Jaws* begat *Piranha* (1978) and *Alligator* (1980), both written by auteur-in-waiting John Sayles while *Alien* (1980) spawned *Humanoids from the Deep* (1981) aka *Monster* and *Galaxy of Terror* (1981). The production designer on the latter film was a certain James Cameron, who would go on to direct the first sequel to Ridley Scott's film in 1986. Another Corman production, Paul Bartel's *Death Race 2000* (1975) may not be a better film than its obvious inspiration *Rollerball* (1974) but it's a lot more fun. Girdler's enthusiastic plundering of other films and popular genres to create something new also seems to anticipate many of the genre films of the 21st century. Ari Aster's extremely accomplished first features, *Hereditary* (2018) and *Midsommar* (2019) riff on the themes and imagery of, respectively, *Rosemary's Baby* (1968) and *The Wicker Man* (1973) and produce something both familiar and oddly disorienting. In the UK, Ben Wheatley's early work does something similar, the sit-com-style gangster story *Down Terrace* (2009) or *Kill List* (2011), an eerie blend of *Get Carter* (1970) and *The Wicker Man*. Quentin Tarantino has made a singular art-form out of such generic mixing and matching, perhaps best displayed in his collaboration with Robert Rodriguez, *Grindhouse* (2007) which fetishistically recreates the 70s cinemagoing experience not only with its double-bill of *Planet Terror* (sci-fi zombies) and *Death Proof* (car-crash serial killer) but also with fake trailers, damaged film stock and missing reels.

Kentucky

William Brent Girdler was born on October 22nd 1947 in Louisville, Kentucky. Friends and collaborators called him Bill. One oft-told story is how he first picked up a film camera aged 5. He was short, 5'5" or 5'6" and musical, with a piano and organ in his house. Most of his films contain a song break and he also worked as a composer and arranger. He often wore a beard or moustache – possibly to look older – and could wear a cowboy hat without looking foolish. Although he came from money, he dressed down. He married for the first time young, aged 17 to Barbara Peter and at the time of his death was married to second wife, Avis. Some people remember him as a Hemingway-esque wild man drawn to danger, others describe him as gentle and soft-spoken but everybody seems to agree that he was obsessed with film and wildly enthusiastic about the projects he took on. Some of his collaborators have suggested his work ethic came from a morbid conviction that he would die young, his grandfather died at 50, his father 40 and, so the story has it, he feared he wouldn't make it past 30.

The Manitou screenwriter Thomas Pope described him as "a street-smart hustler, chubby, cherubic, funny, bold, sassy, and smarter than he knew". Andrew Stevens, who starred in *Day of the Animals* remembered him as, "a gentle and endearing man with a big beard and big passion. He treated cast and crew like family". Girdler was born into one of Louisville's prominent families, his father being Walter H. Girdler Jr, the president of a number of companies including the Girdler Chemical Company (contrary to the myth, he actually died aged 48). As is often the case with film freaks, he caught the bug at an early age. There are frequent mentions in profiles of the director of the cinema he had in the family home and according to some versions of the story, he made his first film aged 8. When he did a stretch in the air force, he was working on training films and honing his technique. His initial foray into the industry was making adverts for Studio One, a company he formed with his brother-in-law J. Patrick Kelly. The company would change its name to Mid-America Pictures in 1973 with Girdler and Kelly being joined by Hugh Smith and Gordon Cornell Layne and all three of them would feature prominently in his story. They moved from ads to feature films, financed partly by Girdler's trust fund. The director would put together a group of loyal collaborators, a number of them family members, many of whom would stay with him throughout his short career.

(Mid-America) will never become MGM, but then I don't want it to. I think we'll be moderately successful. I never expect anything, so I'm never disappointed. I don't claim to be a businessman. All I want to do is make films. (Girdler in Breen 2000-1).

He's been criticized if not dismissed outright by mainstream critics for his unashamed borrowing from other directors and there's been a couple of accusations of credit theft. Hugh Smith, a writer and actor who was a frequent collaborator fell out with the director after he passed off a Smith screenplay as his own work (Smith in Breen 2000-1) although they later patched it up, so much so they were planning further collaborations but fate had other ideas. There's also the controversy around *Asylum of Satan*'s theme song, which is explored in the next chapter. But given the excesses and scandals surrounding a large number of directors from this period, probably Hollywood's last golden age, these accusations are small beer indeed.

His films are shot through with some vague counterculture concerns, the anti-war monologue in *Three on a Meathook*, the post-Watergate paranoia of *Project Kill*, the ecological warning in *Day of the Animals* but it's hard to know if this is a question of politics or a canny exploitation filmmaker surfing the post-hippie *zeitgeist*.

Girdler's career in many ways parallels that of Michael Reeves, the director of three features, the best-known of which is *Witchfinder General* aka *The Conqueror Worm* (1968). Both were born into wealth and fascinated by film from an early age, both started their careers early, learning as they went along. Both were interested in working in popular genres, making films that divided critical opinion and both died young (Reeves died aged 25 in 1969 from what appears to have been an accidental overdose).

Far from Hollywood: Regional Film-making in the 1970s.

It was *Blood Feast* that started it. As director HG Lewis rather fancifully put it, "I've often referred to *Blood Feast* as a Walt Whitman poem. It's no good, but it was the first of its type" (in Palmer 2000:7). Hailed as the first "gore film", Lewis's film tells the story of Fuad Ramses, a psychopathic killer who slaughters women in the name of the ancient Egyptian deity, Isis. Lewis is right, it's not very good but the full color graphic gore (brains being removed, bodies chopped up, a tongue being ripped out) was unlike anything American audiences had seen. The effects are much less convincing than the surgery scenes in the French arthouse horror, *Eyes Without a Face/Les Yeux sans visage* (1960) but Georges Franju's film, even retitled *The Horror Chamber of Dr. Faustus* and double-billed with *The Manster* (1959) for its 1962 US release, had limited appeal to would-be gorehounds, what with its striking stylistic flourishes and cuts made to its more gruesome scenes.

Lewis's film is certainly much less interesting than Herk Harvey's *Carnival of Souls* (1962). An eerie and atmospheric black and white independent shot for $33,000 by a director with a background in industrial films, it's interesting to think how low-budget horror would've developed had Harvey's film made the kind of profits *Blood Feast* did. But despite its technical shortcomings, Lewis delivered on the gore front and consequently his film, which cost less than 25,000, went on to make 4,000,000.

In addition to their subversive content, films like *Night of the Living Dead* (1968), *The Last House on the Left* (1972), *The Texas Chain Saw Massacre* (1974), *I Spit on Your Grave* (1978) and *Friday the 13*[th] (1980) also shared a very similar production lineage: They were made far outside of Hollywood, produced in burgeoning film communities that had sprouted in Florida, Texas, Oregon and New York and all places in between (Albright 2012: 1-2).

The defiant weirdness and poverty-row budgets of many of these films give them a very specific ambience far removed from the Hollywood genre offerings of the period. By way of example, Brian Albright compares SF Brownrigg's bizarre psychodrama *Don't Go in the Basement* (1973), an independent feature made in Texas with the more polished *Race with the Devil*, which was shot in the Lone Star state by a Texan director but financed by 20th Century Fox and with star performers (Peter Fonda, Warren Oates). The impact of the

Sundance Film Festival and break-out hits such as *She's Gotta Have It* (1986) and *Sex, Lies and Videotape* (1989) meant that films that once would have been seen as regional are now instead categorized as independent. But this is really just a matter of branding, Richard Linklater's *Slacker* (1990) was independently made but it's as much of a Texas film as *Don't Look in the Basement* or *The Texas Chainsaw Massacre*. A number of the big indie hits of the 80s and 90s have a determinedly regional quality, whether it be *Sex, Lies and Videotape* (Baton Rouge, Louisiana), *Drugstore Cowboy* (1991, Portland, Oregon) and *Clerks* (1994, Leonardo, New Jersey).

Make no mistake, although these regional horror films of the 70s are often fascinating, quite a lot of them are actually terrible and their technical ineptitude can make even the cheapest indies of the 80s and 90s look polished. But the ineptitude on show does little to dilute that fascination. Brian Albright in his definitive study, *Regional Horror Films 1958 – 90: A State by State Guide* (2012) acknowledges the often shoddy quality of the movies in question. After pointing out how there's "something inherently and almost uniquely American - something downright democratic" about regional horror, he adds:

Which is not to say all of these films are fun to watch. Many of them are quite bad.   Others are passable but clearly made by first-time filmmakers. In some cases, you get the impression that not only have these people never made a film before, it's quite possible they've never *watched* one either' (Albright 2012: 4; emphasis in original).

But alongside the more celebrated work of Romero, Craven and Hooper, there are some unsung gems amidst the dross which are quite unlike anything else out there, films such as *The Other Side of Madness* (1970), *Don't Go in the House* (1980) and *Scarecrows* (1988). As well as providing a training ground for directors who would go on to bigger things (Abel Ferrara, Alan Rudolph, Bob Clark) the regional horror boom also threw up some small-scale auteurs such as Earl Owensby, Charles Pierce and the aforementioned

Brownrigg. There's also no shortage of ambition in many of these films. For Kim Newman, Brownrigg "seems to see himself as a backwoods Bergman and laces his scenario with gratuitous art" (1998:95) and it's true, one person's low-budget slice of exploitation is another's uncompromising artistic statement. *The Last House on Dead End Street* (1978) is a ferocious, startlingly misanthropic take on the Manson case written and directed by a pseudonymous Roger Watkins, who reportedly spend most of the meagre budget on amphetamines. *The Town That Dreaded Sundown* (1978) is a lurid, often blackly comic depiction of the still-unsolved Texarkana Moonlight Murders with the filmmakers assuring us "the incredible story you are about to see is true, where it happened and how it happened; only the names have been changed". There's also a number of films shot in a sunny yet sinister post-Manson California which combine an odd, genuinely dreamlike atmosphere with nightmarish imagery. *Messiah of Evil* aka *Dead People* (1973) is a creepy vaguely Lovecraftian tale of the undead in a small coastal town and offers a fascinating blend of dollar store Antonioni and spooky set pieces which take place in everyday settings such as cinemas and supermarkets. *Warlock Moon* (1973), a story of the occult, ghostly apparitions and cannibalism is also suffused with a very of its time bad trip atmosphere.

The weird hypnotic vibe, the unfamiliar locations and open-ended narratives combined with the visibly low-budgets, the often-terrible acting and the frequent nudity and gore lend a very specific kind of charm to many regional horror films and the fact that many of them are seen in childhood, on poor quality panned-and-scanned video copies or buried in the late night television schedules only adds to their dream-like allure. Some of the first films I saw on VHS were off-beat American indies like *Slithis* aka *Spawn of the Slithis* (1978), *Children Shouldn't Play with Dead Things* (1972) and *Night of the Demon* (1979), not the classic Jacques Tourneur film but a low-budget creature feature which features Bigfoot castrating a urinating biker and whipping another victim with intestines. Chris Haberman sums up the appeal of the latter film:

Is this a "so-bad-it's-good" movie? No. This is one of those rare, largely forgotten films that was taken so seriously by its creators that it is difficult to imagine a large team of people reading the script, enjoying it, coming on-board and putting in the time and energy to bring the terrible story to life. As such this is an "I-must-have-a-fever" movie, because most of what you'll see may feel like a hallucination (2010).

Although there's a massive difference in quality, the good, the bad and the ugly from these cinematic oddities are lodged firmly in my memory and a number of them remain quite unlike anything I've seen in the decades since. William Girdler was another graduate of the regional boom, making his first films far from Hollywood in Louisville. Fellow home-town boy Tod Browning started his film career in New York City before moving to Hollywood and while Girdler too would end up making the move to California, he never entirely left his home state behind. At the time of his death, one of the projects he had lined up was the film that gives this book its title, *Kentucky Wild*.

Chapter 2 - *Asylum of Satan* (1972): Love Slaves of Satan Tortured to Blood-Dripping Death

Synopsis: The film opens on an unexpectedly jarring note for a horror story, with a country and western song, "Red Light Lady", accompanying an ambulance as it cruises through night-time Louisville. Sung by star Nick Jolley, it's the first of a great many seemingly inappropriate musical interludes scattered throughout the director's filmography, an authorial tic as pronounced as Ingmar Bergman's close-ups and Sam Peckinpah's slow-motion mayhem. The ambulance is delivering Lucina Martin (Carla Borelli) to the mansion which houses Pleasant Hill mental hospital. Unaware of why she's been placed there, Lucina finds herself tended to by a German-accented nurse, Martine (who is clearly played, not too convincingly, by a man). When she tries to leave, she is forcibly sedated. Even if one overlooks the weird Martine, there are some pretty obvious clues that this is no normal hospital. In a very spooky scene, Lucina looks out of a window to see patients, white-robed and hooded, sitting in wheelchairs on the lawn. When she visits the dining room, she sits at the only table not occupied by these silent figures, who are unmoving, none of them touching their identical meal of one boiled egg on a plate. She meets some of her fellow patients (the only ones who *aren't* hooded and silent), a woman in a wheelchair, an elderly man and a young blind woman. When they leave, Lucina is alone in the canteen and after being freaked out by freaky Martine, she flees, getting lost in the dimly-lit corridors and hearing the sound of chanting. Meanwhile, her boyfriend, Chris (played by the lumpen stand-up and singer Nick Jolley in a check sports jacket, white trousers, loud tie and massive sideburns) arrives in town and finds out that Lucina is in the hospital. Lucina finally gets to meet Doctor Specter (Charles Kissinger) and he attempts to reassure her that her doctor is behind her admission to Pleasant Hill after she suffered a breakdown. Someone spies on her as she gets undressed and when she bathes, spooky Martine insists on scrubbing her back. When Chris turns up at the hospital, he is told by Specter that he can't see Lucina but our indomitable sports-jacketed hero isn't put off by this and pays a visit to her old doctor. The doctor tells him the transfer to Pleasant Hill was apparently arranged by her father – but Chris informs him that Lucina's father died when she was 12. The doctor also explains that Specter must be elderly, being "in his 70s" when he made his name years ago, although the man Chris met was in early middle-age. All this exposition drives Chris to go to the cops and scenes which serve mainly to dissipate any eerie atmosphere built up, a problem exacerbated by the poor performance of Louis Bandy as Lt. Walsh (Bandy's day job was as salesman for a record company and he acted in his part time):

Chris: There's something wrong with that whole damn place. You feel it. The minute you enter the gates you feel it.

Lt. Walsh: Surely you don't expect us to go out here and raid a place simply because someone has a strange feeling about it. Come on Mr. Duncan, we'd be raiding every church or funeral parlor in town if we used that philosophy.

Back at the hospital, the patients are starting to die, with the wheelchair woman being attacked by bugs in a makeshift gas chamber as a red-lit Specter watches. Another is set on fire, a real letdown compared to the scene in the original screenplay, where he's immolated by green fire that shoots out of a showerhead (see Breen 2000-1 for an analysis of the script). In a truly bizarre sequence, the blind woman is attacked by snakes in a swimming pool. Lt. Walsh and the increasingly desperate Chris head back to Pleasant Hill only to find the place locked up and seemingly abandoned save for a folksy caretaker (Kissinger again) who fobs them off. Chris recognizes him and when he denies being Specter, Chris beats him up. That night in the hospital, Lucina leaves her room to investigate a strange sound and is attacked by a blue-faced ghoul (look closely and you can see the ghoul's false teeth come loose). Hiding in another room, she finds what might be a plaque on the wall and the fast zoom to the year 1803 means we don't get a look at what it is (it would make sense for it to be Specter's medical certificate, indicating what's already been suggested, that he's much older than he appears but it's hard to be sure). The next day, Nick is back at Pleasant Hill and he finally finds proof that something is seriously amiss when he stumbles across the severed head of the blind girl lying in the hospital's dilapidated greenhouse (a sequence which is both horrific and absurd). He wraps it in his jacket and delivers it to the police station, dropping it on Walsh's desk. Walsh has been doing some digging of his own, explaining that Specter died 20 years ago, the suspect in a series of murders before adding how he'd been "picked up several times for devil worship" before lamenting, "We can't go around arresting people for that nowadays". The times have definitely a-changed. In another absurd moment, Walsh shows Chris a color photo of one of Specter's bloody victims and Chris recoils in horror, as if he hadn't just carried a severed head across town. Nick finally convinces Walsh to raid Pleasant Hill. Back at the hospital, the ceremony is about to begin. Lucina, dressed all in white and surrounded by hooded cultists, is tied down, Nurse Martine tears off her mask to reveal Specter (a revelation that really should have come as more of a surprise) and in a hellish red light, the robed and chanting coven prepare to make their sacrifice to Satan. The film ends on an oddly anti-climactic note, partly due to the muffled sound which makes it hard to understand Satan's lines (spoken by Pamela Gatz, who was inside the suit) and so important plot points end up missed. The tension is also diluted by cutting from the ritual to the cops speeding through the night to come to the rescue, although these scenes, set to a funky score seem to anticipate Girdler's *The Zebra Killer*. We are able to work out why the sacrifice goes awry when it turns out Lucina isn't, as Martine puts it, "untouched, unblemished, according to your desire". Early on, we get a flashback to happier times where she and Chris take a walk in snowy woods as foreplay to some coy lovemaking and what initially appears to be a bit of padding turns out to be an important plot point. Satan, presumably angry at being served up the wrong kind of sacrifice, sets Specter on fire. The sense of disorientation isn't helped by the odd coda when, after Specter has been consumed by hellfire and Chris has rescued Lucina, he decides to re-enter the building and appears to glimpse the cult reconstituted. Just before the car drives away, with Chris and Lucina in the back, we get some quick cross-cutting from some red-lit eyes (whose eyes? The driver? Chris?) and the rubbery Satan mask. While the screenplay makes it clear that Chris has been possessed by Specter, as it is it's a muddle, which could charitably be called ambiguous and it also means the film features the *de rigeur* 70s downer endings, the first of many such endings in the director's *oeuvre*.

From the outset of his career, William Girdler was adept at tapping into the *zeitgeist*. While the screenplay was written as *The Asylum of Dr. Death* and the working title was *The Satan Spectrum*, the name of his debut feature cannily combines two popular strands of horror, the madhouse sub-genre and the then-voguish devil movie. Since the shock ending of *Das Cabinet des Dr. Caligari/The Cabinet of Dr. Caligari* (1920), what are now referred to as psychiatric hospitals are a recurring fixture in the horror genre. That combination of an enclosed space and insanity, real or imagined, represent a terrifying loss of control and those in charge of such places, whether it be Caligari, Nurse Ratched or Dr. Lektor are frequently shown to be more dangerous than their charges. Even non-horror films set in such institutions, *The Snake Pit* (1948), *Shock Corridor* (1963) or *Marat/Sade* (1967) contain bizarre and horrific elements. There is clearly a reactionary subtext to a number of these films, the connection between mental illness and violence is not only stigmatizing but it may also discourage people from seeking help (see Rondinone 2019). Writing for the Lancet soon after the premiere of *American Horror Story: Asylum* (2012-13) with its Nazi doctors, aliens, serial killers and lobotomies, Shand, Friedman and Forcen discuss the negative portrayals of both the mentally ill and mental health professionals and wonder if we "can keep the scare but lose the stigma?" (2014). The early 1970s saw a number of such films including the British anthology *Asylum* (1973), the Texas indie *Don't Go in the Basement* aka T*he Forgotten* and the Mexican *La mansion de la locura/The Mansion of Madness* (1973), the latter two being adaptations of the Poe story, *The System of Doctor Tarr and Professor Fether* (1845), a key text in the madhouse horror sub-genre.

Unsurprisingly, the devil has been a recurring fixture in the horror film from the outset but the wave of satanic horror had begun in earnest with the massive success of Roman Polanski's *Rosemary's Baby* (1968). It's isn't hard to see why the satanic horror film was popular in this period, what with the loss of faith in traditional institutions including the church and the growth of alternative belief systems combined with the widespread use of mind-expanding drugs and the death of the utopian hippy dream. 1969 saw a man murdered on camera at the Rolling Stones free concert at Altamont (they opened with "Sympathy for the Devil") and the appearance of icon of evil Charles Manson, whose victims included Polanski's wife, Sharon Tate. In the 70s, it seemed that Satan was everywhere. And in suburban Louisville, his cloven hoof-prints could be seen more clearly than in many other places. According to an article in the *Louisville Courier-Journal* from 1972 entitled Witchcraft:

In a quiet suburban neighborhood, a former Boy Scout who is now a respectable businessman raises a sword and calls for Satan to come forth from Hell. In an old house near the downtown business area, a group of men and women, their nude bodies forming a circle, chants incantations first spoken many centuries before Christ. What they're practicing is witchcraft. The city is Louisville but the same scenes are repeated in Detroit, Kansas City, Dayton, San Francisco, Indianapolis, St. Petersburg and other cities…"Louisville is a center for the occult in the Midwest" said the young man who conducts the weekly witchcraft class at the Free University held at the University of Louisville…"Modern life has gotten to so many people. They feel confused, left out. Witchcraft is an escape from complexities"… Librarians in Louisville reported recently that books on witchcraft are in great demand (Ellis in Aquino 2009: 649).

Did the city's status as satanic hotspot influence Girdler's choice of subject matter or was it just another case of him being attuned to what was going on in the wider world? Kissinger's Specter is portrayed as urbane and like many a screen Satanist, with his neatly-trimmed (if obviously stuck-on) goatee and pirate shirt, he comes over as a bit of a fop. Aleister Crowley's bisexuality may well be the source of this particular trope, which can also be seen at work in films such as *Night of the Demon* (1957) and *The Devil Rides Out* (1968). The Church of Satan's Anton LaVey's may have claimed (repeatedly) that he played a part in the making of *Rosemary's Baby* but that seems to have another example of LaVeyan self-mythologizing. Presumably inspired by these stories, the film credits the Church of Satan as "technical consultant" with LaVey's right-hand man, Michael Aquino, helping with the ritual scenes. Aquino is a fascinating character, a former political scientist who would go on to break with LaVey in 1975 and form his own occult group The Temple of Set. The way he tells it, Studio One contacted him because they "wanted to outdo Brotherhood of Satan", a creepy story of soul transference made a year before *Asylum*. Aquino explains how "the Church of Satan was invited to review the setting and script of the ritual sequence and to coach the actor-satanists and the demon in their behavior" (Aquino 2009:175). Despite this expert help the ritual scenes are not all that different to the ones in a host of other devilish movies, billowing incense clouds, robes, chants, organ music, candles and a bound and gagged Lucina laid out on the altar. Aquino was proud enough of his contribution to include a couple of pages of the script in his book, *The Church of Satan* (2009). The fact that Specter plays the organ may also be a nod to the musician-turned-diabolist LaVey. There is a real chill in the presentation of the ritual as a form of macabre surgery and the murky cinematography is even more striking with everything lit up in blood-red. Specter's speech clarifies things for viewers who haven't been paying attention:

We are about to meet again, master. I've kept our pact these many years, the mute was burned, the blind girl was given to the reptiles and beheaded, the cripple was fed to the insects. Now, master, you will soon have your sacrifice.

Martine's pronouncements are even more hyperbolic ("loose the hounds from the barrier and come among us…Hail Satan!") but the long-awaited appearance of the devil himself is a real let-down. The costume was, according to members of the crew, borrowed from the Polanski film (see Breen 2000-1) and it certainly looks like the suit we get glimpses of in Rosemary's dream sequence but the effect is muted when it's combined with the cheap mask, which is silly rather than scary. It's not clear how the director managed to get his hands on the suit or indeed, what happened to it after the film but Aquino seems to confirm its provenance in a section of his book where he dispels any Polanski/La Vey connection:

As far as the Devil-suit of fur and scales, it was flown to Louisville, Kentucky in 1971 for use in a horror film (Asylum of Satan) being shot there for which I was a technical advisor (Aquino 2009:37).

He also confirms that the suit was so small, only a skinny female could fit it into it. Girdler may have acquired it through the Hollywood connections that, according to persistent rumor, he had even in those early days in Louisville. Michael Kohnhorst, a photojournalism student from Western Kentucky University who was a photographer on the *Asylum* shoot has written how "Our Writer/Producer/Director/ Editor and Composer, William Girdler, had ingratiated himself with many established Hollywood filmmakers, and our crew was star struck when we were visited by Charles G. Clark, a retired Hollywood cinematographer whose career had begun in 1915. We were mesmerized by his stories and intrigued by his prediction that some of us might have careers making motion pictures" (Kohnhorst undated). Clark, who had worked on films from the prestigious likes of Andre De Toth (*Slattery's Hurricane* [1949]), Richard Fleischer (*Violent Saturday* [1955]) and John Huston (*The Barbarian and the Geisha* [1958]) was right about Kohnhorst, who would go on to work as a director of photography on *The Grudge 2* (2006) and the remake of the legendary regional horror film, *The Town that Dreaded Sundown* (2014). The fact that animals, be it snakes or bugs, figure prominently in a couple of killings prefigures Girdler's later 'nature gone wild' films, *Grizzly* and *Day of the Animals*. These murders are imaginatively staged while also being remarkably restrained by the standards of early 70s horror, as is the lovemaking between Lucina and Chris (possibly as a result of Borelli's reluctance to do nude scenes).

Asylum is primitive, visibly underfunded (with a paltry budget of $50,000 – $70, 000) and stilted. But there's an appealing chilly atmosphere, the grey skies, skeletal trees and the imposing setting (the exteriors of the hospital were, in reality, a mansion overlooking the Ohio River built by the Ballards, a prominent Louisville family). There are also some effectively creepy moments and the atmosphere in the asylum – Lucina's oddly homely room, the robed and hooded patients, those boiled eggs – is appropriately nightmarish.

Like so many of the director's films, *Asylum of Satan* was a family affair. Girdler's brother-in-law J. Patrick Kelly produced and co-wrote the screenplay and several members of what would become his stock company make an appearance. Carla Rueckert is uncredited as a cult member but would go on to *The Zebra Killer* and an off-screen role as a researcher on *Abby* while Sherry Steiner, the "Blind Girl" would play the female lead in the director's next film. Although the director couldn't afford stars, he could feature a famous face, albeit only in Louisville. Claude Wayne Fulkerson was known for pitching used cars and soda pop in TV ads but he presumably came to the director's attention more for his appearances as Peter Gory (a play on Peter Lorre), a 60s horror host. Surprisingly he's very good as a sinister orderly with a DA haircut and sideburns. He also pops up in a memorable cameo in *Abby* but his only post-Girdler credit is in something called *The Fated Assemblage of Dr Malvoglio* (2013). A story about a plan to open the gates of hell, it not only features characters called Rosemary, Fulci, Roeg and "Brian Palmer", it casts Fulkerson as Dr. Martin Lucina. Writer/director/star Beau Kaelin is clearly a fan of Girdler's debut.

Carla Borelli, who plays Lucina was the only cast member with serious screen credits, having appeared in some popular TV shows including *77 Sunset Strip* (1958 – 64), *The Wild Wild West* (1965 – 9) and *Ironside* (1967 – 75). She also turned up in the TV movie *Ritual of Evil* (1970) where she yet again fell prey to satanists (that time round, she didn't survive). *Asylum*'s unlikely hero figure, Chris is played by Nick Jolley in his only film. Better known as a minor Broadway actor he's an unappealing lead in some startlingly bad outfits, a lot of clashing plaid. The most interesting performers in the film would become well-known to fans of the director. James Carroll Pickett aka Jim Pickett was another native of Louisville who started as a theater actor. Like many Girdler collaborators, he was versatile and resourceful, not only appearing as the blue-faced, bloody-mouthed ghoul who attacks Lucina (what the character is doing there remains unclear) but also providing some of the make-up effects. After making three films with Girdler, two of them as a main player, Pickett stopped acting and moved to California in the mid-70s, reinventing himself as an award-winning playwright. He was the writer in residence at the Beverly Hills Playhouse and also became known for his activism, becoming the co-founder of Artists Confronting Aids. His play *Dream Man* was filmed in 1991 but like too many of the director's collaborators, Pickett didn't live long, dying of AIDS aged 44 in 1994.

Directors often work repeatedly with the same lead actor and film history is full of examples of enduring teams, be it Johns Ford and Wayne, Scorsese and De Niro or Herzog and Kinski. The closest thing Girdler had to John Wayne was Charles Kissinger. Like Fulkerson, he was a minor celebrity in Louisville for his appearances as the Fearmonger, a horror host on the local station WDRB-TV. Horror Hosts were a very American thing and an important part of genre history, introducing old black and white features to a young, often would-be hip audiences, many of whom would become known as Monster Kids. While some hosts such as Vampira, Elvira and Zacherley would become well-known, many of these hosts would be local performers on regional channels and much of their work has been lost over time. Unlike the bigger names who had costumes and sets, the Fearmonger's look was defiantly lo-fi with Kissinger merely holding a torch under his chin. The result was undoubtedly effective and there were also some primitive special effects used to float his disembodied head. Like other hosts including Fulkerson's Gory, the Fearmonger was primarily a comic figure, delivering horror-themed gags in the ad breaks for the films. The films themselves were typical late night horror fare from that period, a mixture of Universal titles, some of the milder Hammer films and some 50s science fiction although WDRB's programming was unusual in that it played its double-bills in the early evening (from 7pm to 10pm) and this doubtless exposed Kissinger's act to a much younger crowd than was usual. No footage or audio of the Fearmonger is known to exist but there are loving testaments to the character on genre websites. *Asylum of Satan* is an ideal showcase for Kissinger, his three roles displaying his versatility and he especially shines given some of the weaker performances on display (poor acting is so often an element in the low-budget regional horrors of the period). Kissinger would appear in seven of Girdler's nine films, often in a leading role and poignantly, his movie career would end with the director's untimely death, although he would continue live performance and making ads.

The film also marked Girdler's first collaboration with any of the Asman brothers, three Louisville natives who would work in different capacities on most of the director's features. William aka Bill Asman was the cinematographer on the director's first 4 features, returning for *Grizzly* before going on to have a long career as a camera operator. Sound man John Asman came on board for *Meathook* and would make another 5 Girdler features before working mainly in TV. Bub aka Bob aka Henry Asman would have an even more distinguished filmography, editing six of the director's features before going on to sound-editing and a long working relationship with Clint Eastwood. To date, he's won 2 Oscars.

Seventeen-year-old Don Wrege was an aspiring musician who got a gig working on *Asylum* as a clapboard operator. Along with his friend Christopher Lee (not that one) he wrote the opening song "Red Light Lady" at Girdler's behest and the duo recorded it. At the premiere they were sanguine that their song had been re-recorded by what Wrege calls ""real" musicians" but were shocked to see it credited to the director. When he told his story to the William Girdler website at the turn of the century, he seemed philosophical:

I didn't mention it when I saw Girdler at a wedding a couple of years later. I was two years through film school at this point and asked him what he was working on. "A turkey called 'Three on a Meathook'," I think he replied. I clearly remember him saying "turkey," because as a dedicated, self-centered artiste of a filmmaker halfway through film school I was deeply offended. I nearly threw what was left of my drink on him, but controlled myself. I figured if he had a career in Hollywood and I didn't, why should I insult him? Perhaps he'd take advantage of me again? After all, wasn't that how people got ahead in Hollywood? So I have always recounted Girdler stealing my stolen song as "becoming a professional" at the tender age of 17 (Wrege in Breen 2000-1).

But speaking to me a couple of decades later, his opinion of the film and its director had soured considerably:

In my opinion as a film school graduate, it's embarrassingly bad on a level that transcends mockery. The horror in this film is that it was released at all. With his "musical" contribution (i.e. mine and Chris'), his co-writing of the script and his directorship, Girdler obviously viewed himself as a renaissance man. in reality he was a marginally talented spoiled kid with a lot of money to play with.

Having started a production company – and having big dreams – Girdler was firmly attuned to the business side of the industry. Like many a maker of regional horror films, he decided to play up his hometown roots and decided to get a local newspaper, *The Courier-Journal* in on the act. In November 1971 there was a set report headlined, "Devilish Doings, Cinematic satan stalks Louisville area; his motive is profit", where Girdler and Kelly talk about the plans to make the city "a natural center for films – as natural as California. The climate is pleasant a good percentage of the year… Within a 300-mile radius of Louisville is terrain duplicating nearly every kind of terrain in Western Europe so we can do European-type films here" (Kelly in Long 1971). A month later on December 5th staff writer Lana Ellis (the same Lana Ellis who wrote about occult Louisville) offered a valuable first-hand account of the process behind Girdler's debut feature – and her part in it. Her story was titled, "Horrors! Or how I lost my hopes for an Oscar (not to mention my false eyelashes) while playing a hooded figure in a low-budget, Louisville-made fright flick":

I'd missed my chance to be the bride of Dracula or a teen-age werewolf but there was still hope. A full-length horror movie was being filmed in Louisville and there was a part for me in it. I was excited. Horror flicks are big sellers now, even better than the sexploitation films. Even a production that's not up to Academy Award standards has a good shot at being booked into drive-ins. Thus, the backers turn a tidy profit and unknown actors get to ply their trade and hope that, although most of their audiences will be more intent on popcorn and backseat sex maybe someone important will catch the performance. Sure, it's a humble beginning but look what happened to Vincent Price (Ellis 1971).

Cast as a member of Specter's coven she first has to lose her black underwear (in case it shows through the white robes), tie back her hair and get rid of her jewelry. She's part of a 22 person crew and 15 person cast. There's a wry, slightly mocking tone to her piece but she offers valuable insight into the unpretentious vibe, what with star Jolley telling her, "What we lack in money, we make up in heart" (Ellis 1971). There are some errors in the piece but it's hard to know if these are, in fact, teasers from Girdler and Kelly. Ellis's description of the plot, as told to her by Carla Borelli, sounds even more lurid than the real thing:

She (Borelli) plays a girl who has the bad taste to fall in love with a young man who has sold his soul to the devil. In exchange for immortality and trading stamps or whatever it is the devil gives his buddies, her boyfriend must go around killing people. As far as I can figure, I'm one of the past victims who have now formed a mumbling, ghostly Greek chorus" (Ellis 1971).

She gets Steiner mixed up with Girdler's sister Lynne Kelly, reporting that the latter gets "the plum role" of being attacked by snakes in a swimming pool but this confusion may be because it was Kelly who stepped in to play Steiner's death scene. The "three live boa constrictors" seems to be pure invention on the part of the filmmakers, as does the claim that "the movie does have some weird scenes, like the ones in which a woman is done in by 1,000 insects and in which a cripple and a deaf-mute are sacrificed to the Devil" (Ellis 1971). A thousand? Girdler and Kelly sell themselves as both businessmen and artists, paying close attention to both aspects of the film business:

From an artistic standpoint, the film is being made with one simple objective. "To scare the hell out of people", said Girdler. "There's no sex, no blood and guts", he said. He describes the film as the Gothic type of horror movie. "We leave the 'gross' scenes at the point where the mind can take over", said Girdler (Ellis 1971).

You wouldn't think it would be too hard to promote a film with such a lurid title but for some unknown reason, many of the ads foregrounded the weakest aspect, that boggle-eyed fright mask. The trailer however, is a truly remarkable bit of exploitation marketing with a montage of images, including most of the gore, set to a funky soundtrack and accompanied by an incredibly florid voiceover:

Pleasant Hill Hospital, for those on the outside peaceful and serene, for those on the inside filled with terror and evil beyond belief. A beautiful girl, torn from the arms of love, her very life a nightmare in the house of hell with no hope of escape or mercy… awakened by a mutilated crazed animal who seeks her beauty to appease the blood lust of a devil bridegroom pursued to the canyons of hell to the edge of sanity by the bestial cravings of the Prince of Darkness.

The director staged the World Premiere on September 26th at the Vogue cinema in his hometown, where it was described as "the first full-length motion picture produced and filmed entirely in Louisville with an All-Louisville cast" (Reed in Harris 2020). Given that they'd been involved almost from the start *The Courier-Journal* was there with the headline "The World Premiere of `Asylum of Satan` Perks Up a Dull Tuesday". Reporter Billy Reed describes the scene:

The first person in line was Wade Connick, 3912 Elfin Avenue. Connick sported a trim blond moustache and he was carrying an umbrella, lest a downpour came while he waiting to buy a ticket. Connick said he had been at the theater since 6:45 [the film started at 8:00]…When the doors finally opened the crowd filed slowly into the theater, passing on the way the members of the cast who were clustered on the sidewalk, smoking cigarettes and generally looking semi-nervous. The actors wore tuxedos, just like they do at the big premieres out in Hollywood and the women wore a colorful variety of clinging, low-cut, low-cut, floor-length gowns. It was not Graumann's Chinese but it was a worthy try (Ibid.).

As Girdler must have suspected the biggest reaction from the audience was toward Claude Fulkerson:

In the movie he plays the evil doctor's assistant but most of the fans recognized him as the star of the Big Red soda commercial. "Ok, Look, it's HIM" screamed one matron. "No, it can't be…by golly it IS him" said her companion (Ibid.)

The few reviews were poisonous. Anna Calvert, the reviewer for another Louisville paper, *The Voice-Jeffersonian*, was (pardon the pun) damning, as indicated by the title of her review, ""Satan" is just a devilishly awful movie":

I'm not a devotee of horror flicks. So I probably would have skipped 'Asylum of Satan' had it not been that I had watched some of it being filmed last November on the Schmutz estate in Glenview… As a matter of fact, if this incredibly amateurish movie gets much circulation it might well sabotage years of work our Chamber of Commerce has spent in improving Louisville's image around the country… At that point [the snake-in-the-pool murder] it was clear that Girdler was having the most fun with his horror effects. When the film switched to a 'Love Story' sequence, the sudden change and imitation of better films cracked me up completely. With each film attempt at reminiscing, the laughter became louder. When it was over, finally it seemed a pity that local people had to pay $2 to view Studio 1's attempt at a feature-length home movie. On the set, they had enjoyed their work and took themselves very seriously – security police and the whole bit…It is as well that it is playing at a drive-in, because that atmosphere gives viewers an opportunity to do other things when the movie drops to its worst points. But to be captive at the Vogue Matthews for such a movie, is a waste of time and money and I can't help but be dumbstruck by the people who have the guts to foist such trash upon the public…By the end of the final reel it seems as if (and the story line is never very clear about such details) everyone in "Asylum" has gone to the devil. So has this wretched movie (Calvert 1972).

The second World Premiere (?!) took place three days later and this was marketed much more cannily. As well as the "FREE Sign of Satan Soul Protector given out to each person! Protects from the Star of the Devil" (it was actually just a button badge), Girdler used the bad reviews in the publicity, proudly announcing:

Louisville's Most Controversial Film. Critics Slam it Unmercifully, The Public Disagrees and Rebels. You Must See and Decide for Yourself.

The British indie horror director Pete Walker had done something similar to publicize his *Frightmare* (1974) and David Lynch would use the "Two Thumbs Down" from Siskel and Ebert to market *Lost Highway* (1994). The event also offered a firework show but not just any fireworks, these were "Satan's Gigantic Fireworks". As if that wasn't enough, there was also screenings of *Dr. Frankenstein* (1970, a retitling of a Canadian feature called *Dr. Frankenstein on Campus*), *Night of the Witches* (1970) and perennial favorite *Night of the Living Dead* (1968). For anyone interested in the rural filmmaking tradition, it's interesting just how prominently the hometown connection was emphasized, "Produced in Louisville! Filmed in Louisville! Starring Louisville Actors!"

A recent bit on the film in the *Louisville Magazine* makes clear that although it's remembered, it's still not really admired. Unambiguously titled, "This Terrible, Locally Filmed Horror Movie Is Our New Halloween Tradition", authors Dylan Jones and Josh Moss remind us that:

Forty-seven years ago, on Sept. 26, 1972, *Asylum of Satan* premiered at the Vogue Theater in St. Matthews. The movie, shot by the late Louisville filmmaker William Girdler at a Glenview estate, riled up *Courier-Journal* critic William Mootz…The guess-you-could-call-it-a-plot: A woman arrives at "Pleasant Hill Hospital" (spoiler: IT'S ACTUALLY THE ASYLUM OF SATAN) and her fiancé attempts to rescue her. Highpoints include sinister air vents, sinister pipe organs, sinister goatees, sinister French accents, sinister close-ups of candles, sinister cross-dressing. And the calmest reaction in the history of motion pictures to a severed head being delivered on a police detective's desk (Jones and Moss 2019).

Girdler fan and Louisville native Tyler Harris is more generous, pinpointing just what it is about the film that works for some of us:

Amidst the mix of occasionally phony, occasionally effective horror, lined along all the fake water snakes and crawling bugs and devil make-up falsely purported to have been stolen from the set of

Rosemary's Baby there really is heart. And there's merit. And there's love. And that's clearly the Girdler touch (Harris 2020).

***Body Shop* aka *Doctor Gore*: Filmed in a Laboratory so evil… it makes Dr. Frankenstein's workshop look like a nursery.**

Bill Girdler had a beautiful organ in his living room in Louisville. He played it well. One day, just after he played a grand piece for me, I said "Okay, now everyone skate the other way!" It angered him and, of course, I apologized (David Sheldon).

Directed by JG Patterson Jr, this low-budget take on Frankenstein is included here on the basis of its score, composed and performed by Bill Girdler. Patterson, who had the striking birth name of Jr. Junius Gustavious Patterson had a touring magic/spook show and his special effects work can be seen in the H.G. Lewis films, *She Devils on Wheels* (1968) and *Just for the Hell of It* (1968). He'd also, like Kissinger and Fulkerson, worked as a horror host, appearing as "Mad Daddy" on a Charlotte, North Carolina channel in the late 50s. *Body Shop* was his directorial debut and it's a bit of a one man show, he wrote the script and, credited as Don Brandon "America's No. 1 Magician", also appears as the title character. The film is aimed squarely at the *Blood Feast* crowd, being an amateurish mess with primitive production values which nevertheless manages to provide the required lashings of gore. At one stage thought to be lost, it was released on video cassette in the early 80s along with an intro from the Godfather of Gore himself, Lewis. He comes over as an avuncular salesman, albeit one…who keeps…taking long… pauses as he talks about "my friend Pat Patterson". He explains the fake blood rule, that the goriness of a film can be measured by how many gallons are used. So *Blood Feast* was a 3 gallon picture, *Two Thousand Maniacs!* (1964) a 5 gallon picture but the films he made with Patterson upped the blood considerably to 15 – 20 gallons. He more or less warns us:

Don't look for highly sophisticated film-making here, if ever a film were made by one person and is a reflection of one person, it's this film. You may not like the acting, you may not like the storyline, for all I know you may not like the gore but I think you'll agree after you've seen this picture you're not about to forget it.

It really isn't very good, with Patterson's "Don Brandon" playing a character called Don Brandon, a plastic surgeon whose glamorous wife Anitra is killed in an accident. Along with his hunchbacked. Igor-ish assistant, he attempts to revive her corpse with stolen body parts, the fact that Brandon is a most unlikely babe magnet ensuring that there's a ready supply of nubile would-be victims. It's a slipshod affair, from the thunder sound effects added to shots of a rain-free blue sky or the low-fi experiments performed with tinfoil and duct tape. There's also little attention paid to cinematic technique, what with the overlighting of most of the scenes and the static camera. We even get a glimpse of the clapperboard in one shot. The gore is fairly effective, in that HG Lewis vaguely clinical, very bloody fashion with Brandon removing a leg, arms and eyes. There's a stilted, repetitive quality to it which could charitably be described as dreamlike as well as a Girdler-style musical interlude, a country song from Bill Hicks (not the late comedian but rather a barrel-chested Burl Ives lookalike). Half-way through, the film changes tack and becomes a weird kind of male fantasy with Brandon courting and cavorting with his rejuvenated and hypnotized bride. She's presented as a beautiful but child-like living sex doll and there's something very creepy about the moment Brandon tells her, "You have so much to learn, so much I must teach you" as the Wedding March plays on the organ. There follows a montage of the couple doing romantic things interspersed with woozy flashbacks to his operations (a sequence which is all the more startling after more than an hour of flat presentation). But it doesn't work out, with Anitra making a move on Brandon's assistant, who gets a face full of acid from the doctor while she cuddles a pet rabbit. She then seduces a lumpen tradesman with this exchange:

Anitra: "You're a man.

Tradesman: "You sure ain't".

Anitra: "No, I'm a woman".

In a damp squib ending, Brandon ends up behind bars while Anitra rides off into the sunset with a passing motorist. It's possible Patterson is trying to say something about the male desire to remake women and the dangers therein but *Vertigo* (1958) this ain't. It is though, as Lewis suggests, an interesting reflection of Patterson's psyche, what with every woman finding him irresistible and yet, in a weird coda, a woman he blew off earlier turns up to see him in prison, accompanied by her new boyfriend. This character is played by Patterson's real-life wife Nita (a name very like Anitra). But this makes it sound more interesting than it is.

Girdler's contribution is not really distinctive, especially when compared to his effectively spare electronic score for his second feature *Three on a Meathook*. The theme is a variation on "My Favorite Things" (the copyright lawyers must have missed this one) with some banal lyrics:

"Sugar and spice and everything nice, that's what little girls are made of.

But as they get bigger they take on a figure and some are much nicer than others."

The operation scenes are largely wordless and the tinny organ accompaniment plays throughout like muzak. Patterson's film offers a useful comparison to Girdler's early work, which is certainly underbudgeted and sometimes slipshod but never as fundamentally inept or uninspired. Indeed, as Alexandra Heller-Nicholas wrote about *Wrong Way* (1972), a sleazy Wes Craven rip-off:

To those unfamiliar with grindhouse aesthetics, *The Last House on the Left* may appear to be as crude as cinema productions can get, but when compared to *Wrong Way*, it demonstrates moments of genuine artistry (2011:84).

In much the same way, those critics who find the likes of *Asylum of Satan* and *The Zebra Killer* to be barely competent may find it instructive to sit through *un film de* Pat Patterson. The advertising for *Doctor Gore* is, even by the standards of exploitation films of the period, over the top. Alongside some primitive sketches of skeletons, a terrified woman and a torture scene, the poster boasts not only the tagline used here as a sub-heading but also promises "You'll forget about The Godfather and Mark of the Devil when you see…The Body Shop" adding "No-one should see it alone…4 Dimensions in Horror, extreme realism…Horror beyond belief…No-one should see it alone…in thrilling color…psycho-shock technique…". If that isn't enough of a warning/promise, at the bottom of the poster we're told:

This motion picture is not reccomended (sic.) for impressionable children or adults or anyone with mental problems, heart trouble or just bad nerves! Check with your doctor if you have any doubts! You see it at your own risk!

The ads for the home video release managed, incredibly, to be even more hyperbolic, describing the film as:

Censored for your own sanity! Warning: Before watching this special film, ask yourself "Am I mentally stable enough to withstand one mind-shattering shock after another?"

Patterson continued to work in the low-budget drive-in arena, directing the even more obscure *The Electric Chair* (1976) and producing the highly regarded cult movie *Axe* (1974) aka *Lisa, Lisa* aka *The California Axe Massacre* before dying aged only 45 of malignant melanoma.

He would repay the favor to Girdler, providing the special effects for the director's next feature, another low-budget horror film but this time inspired by a real-life case of murder and mutilation.

Chapter 3 - *Three on a Meathook* (1972): A Padlocked Shed, Hooks of Cold Steel – a Maniac on the Loose

Synopsis: In an apartment block in Louisville, a couple have just finished an afternoon sex session. The naked young woman tells her partner about her upcoming trip "to the lake" with her friends, the opening scene delivering a text-book example of the exploitation arena's seamless blend of minimal exposition and exposed female flesh. We then follow the four friends on their trip, which mainly consists of a lengthy skinny-dipping scene, interrupted by a young man passing in a canoe, his arrival accompanied by some ominous music cues (Girdler's score is very good throughout, a blend of jarring synth and wah wah guitar). That night, near midnight, the group's car breaks down and a truck arrives, driven by that same young man, who introduces himself as Billy Townsend (played by Girdler regular James Pickett). He's reluctant to leave them there "the way things are nowadays" and offers them a place to stay. Billy's Pa, Frank (Charles Kissinger, another familiar face) is clearly upset, taciturn and hostile and his mood only darkens as he sits up in bed drinking whisky and listening to the laughter of the girls. Later that night one of the girls is taking a bath when an unseen intruder enters and stabs her to death. Then the intruder attacks the others, killing two of them with shotgun blasts. One manages to escape and she runs around the house, trying to phone for help before she's beheaded (in a really eye-opening moment).

The next morning Billy is horrified to discover the women dead but Frank is the very model of reassurance, giving his son money to go and see a movie and telling him he "will take care of everything, it's going to be alright" (a line he repeats in that eerily soft-spoken monotone). Billy goes to visit his mother's grave and talks to her before heading into the city. There we get a typical Girdler *verité* portrait of night-time Louisville, all neon and speeding cars as Billy leaves the cinema (showing a re-release of *The Graduate*) and ends up in a bar watching a band in matching outfits play a couple of songs. There's something jarring about the moment a waitress approaches Billy, telling him expressionlessly, "You've got a big problem, haven't you?" The waitress, Sherry (Sherry Steiner) turns out to have a heart of gold but her flat affect and unusual pronunciation lend her scenes an odd, distanced quality (she has the same spacey presence in *Asylum of Satan* but it works better for an inmate in a psychiatric hospital than it does a cocktail waitress). Billy gets drunk and wakes up the next day in Sherry's bed and although she is naked, she reassures him that they didn't have sex. She also tells him that he kept mumbling, "I couldn't have done it" in his sleep. Her obvious romantic interest in him appears to be undimmed by the fact that he was so intoxicated he wet the bed (it's glaringly obvious that Sherry is the forgiving sort). The two spend some time together walking and sitting in a playground (a scene which calls to mind the interplay between the lovers in *Asylum of Satan*) and he tells her, in what will turn out to be an important bit of exposition, that he's only recently come back to the family farm after spending time in Ohio. Before he leaves, Billy invites Sherry and a friend to come out to the farm that weekend. Arriving home, Frank is clearly upset and Billy's newfound confidence – and the news that they're going to have visitors – makes their already tense relationship a good deal frostier. That night Billy is unable to sleep and is tormented by a traumatic flashback to his childhood. He's riding a bike through the fields, an image that would be idyllic if it wasn't for that ominous soundtrack. He walks into the house to find Frank standing over the bleeding corpse of a young woman before he asks his son, "What have you done?" The next morning, Sherry and her friend Becky arrive at the farm and again, the images are pleasant, the trio horsing around and walking through the overgrown fields. This time Frank is not only taciturn but clearly drunk and the moment he dishes out the bread for dinner, tossing a slice onto each plate in turn, is a masterclass in barely concealed disdain. The women do their best to engage Frank in conversation about the meat they're eating (which they're told is veal) and Frank informs them, "it depends on what parts you use as to how it's cut". After the meal, Becky goes to bed, leaving Billy and Sherry alone and they have sex on the sofa. Upstairs, Frank enters Becky's room and kills her with a pickaxe. The next morning, Sherry goes looking for Becky, visiting a series of dilapidated outhouses and in an isolated smokehouse she discovers the bodies of three semi-naked women hanging on meathooks. Understandably horrified, she runs back to the farmhouse and rushes into the kitchen where she finds Frank cutting up a human leg. When she asks him what he's doing, he tells her, "Making dinner". Frank attacks Sherry, Billy appears and tries to stop him and as the two men struggle, an old woman suddenly rushes wordlessly into the room and ends up with Frank's cleaver stuck in her back. Billy recognizes her right away ("Mama?") and Frank implores his son with the now familiar, "What have you done?" The film ends with a psychiatrist providing Billy and Sherry an explanation for what we've already worked out, Billy's mother not being dead but hidden away while Billy was in Ohio due to her being "ill, terribly ill…the nature of her illness was cannibalistic". The move from caretaker to executioner was too much for Pa's mind and just as Norman convinced himself that Mother was alive, so Frank started to believe that Billy was a killer. The last shot is of Frank, straitjacketed behind bars and hopelessly insane.

Far more than a gruesome knockoff, *Three on a Meathook* is a moving testament to creative professionals who, faced with a cheap premise and limited resources, made an unlikely work of art, capturing the best and worst of the human experience (Padua 2020).

Girdler's second feature has attained a measure of fame for that (admittedly excellent) title, a play on words inspired either by the superstition (it's unlucky to be the third person to get a light from the same match) or the Mervyn Le Roy pre-code film, *Three on a Match* (1932). The film is clearly a riff on Hitchcock or more precisely, a series of riffs, starting with the central premise. In *Psycho* we're led to believe Mrs. Bates is responsible for Norman's murders whereas in *Meathook*, it's the parent who's the killer, not the son. Both Norman and Frank are depicted as enablers motivated by love but they're really only covering up their own crimes. And yet Girdler adds *another* twist, imagining what would have happened if Mrs. Bates really had been hidden away in the fruit cellar still alive. The revelation that Frank is killing young women not for kicks but in to supply his cannibal wife with human flesh is a demented touch which gives the film one of its wildest moments, the sudden entry of the silent old woman as Billy tries to protect Sherry from a cleaver-wielding Frank followed by her sudden death. It's like something out of an EC comic, a twist as bizarre as it is absurd. But it isn't just about the plot, the twin specters of Hitch and Mrs. Bates haunt the whole film. It opens with a shot clearly riffing on the opening of *Psycho* as the camera pans across a cityscape to fix on an apartment building and zoom in one window and in the room there's a couple enjoying a daytime tryst *a'la* Marion and Sam.

A shot of one of Billy's unfortunate female guests silhouetted in a window conjures up a similar image of Mrs. Bates and Billy's vocal response to the bloody aftermath of the massacre can't help but remind us of Norman's reaction to that shower stall. Billy's visit to his mother's grave right after is another tease and his communing with her in a tremulous voiceover is pure Norman. The scene where he, after spending the night with Sherry, is ordered to wash his hands by his Pa ("your Ma always demanded clean hands") is also presumably another nod to Hitchcock, the boy having sullied himself by associating with women who aren't his mother. This is underlined by Frank's prayer before the meal, "Bless this boy and keep his evil doings in the past. Bless our Ma". The shock moments, the decapitation, Becky's gruesome death by pickaxe, owe less to the celebrated shower scene and more to the death of Detective Arbogast, dispatched on the stairs in a sudden eruption of violence.

Any pretense of merely riffing on/paying homage to Hitchcock's best-known film is abandoned by the end, where Girdler lifts the two climactic scenes wholesale, the explanatory speech from the psychiatrist and Frank alone in a cell, wearing a straitjacket as he delivers a monologue in voice-over. Perhaps wisely there's no attempt to recreate one of the most chilling images in the Master's *oeuvre*, Mother's skeletal face superimposed over that of Norman.

Robert Bloch's source novel *Psycho* (1959) was famously inspired by the case of the "Plainfield Ghoul" Ed Gein (1906 – 1984), the mother-fixated murderer and grave-robber who fashioned grotesque art out of pilfered body parts (his possessions included leggings made of skin, a corset made from a woman's torso, a shoebox full of female genitals and a belt adorned with nipples). The fact that Gein fashioned clothing out of human skin and *décor* out of bones was considerably toned down by Bloch and his Norman is content just to dress in his late mother's clothes. Girdler was uncannily prescient in revisiting the Gein case and injecting more nastiness than Bloch or Hitchcock could (including referencing the oft-told rumors than Gein was a cannibal), anticipating the even more graphic takes that were to soon follow. The remarkable *The Texas Chain Saw Massacre* (the title of which gives *Meathook* a run for its money) would also focus on isolated rural folk and their habit of turning unwary humans into meals. But Hooper's film, for all its apocalyptic flair and nightmare logic, could only offer us One on a Meathook. The impressive *Deranged* (1974) stuck closer to the facts of the case, as would the later *In the Light of the Moon* aka *Ed Gein* (2013). Later Gein-esque killers can be found in *The Silence of the Lambs* (1991) and *American Horror Story: Asylum*. Indeed, while Charles Manson may have been portrayed in more films, especially the strain of low-budget pulp movies I've referred to elsewhere as "Mansonsploitation" (see Cooper 2018), Gein has the unusual distinction of inspiring some of the best-known horror films ever made.

There's also the noteworthy use of the subjective camera to represent the killer's point-of-view. There's just such a shot in a later scene with the uncomfortable dinner served up by the whisky-soaked Frank observed through a window but it's unclear if this time round it's the point-of-view of the cannibal Mama or if it's just a kind of cinematographic red herring, suggesting an unseen killer to heighten what's already a pretty tense scenario. But the use of the technique as the killer makes his way to the room where the women are staying is uncannily prescient. The point-of-view shot was by no means new, Abel Gance used it in *Napoleon* (1927) and the noir *Lady in the Lake* (1947) uses the device throughout (as would the later *Enter the Void* [2009] and the remake of *Maniac* [2012]. But it would become familiar to the point of tedium in the slasher cycle of the late 70s. After years of knowing, semi-parodic reflexive variants *(Scream* [1996 – date]) and TV shows that riff on the format (*American Horror Story: 1984* [2019], *Fear Street* [2021), it's instructive to consider just how lowbrow and critically despised the humble slasher movie was before the injection of all that irony. Siskel and Ebert devoted a much-discussed episode of their film review show in 1980 attacking the likes of *Don't Go in the House* and *Friday the 13*[th] and predictably, the question of point-of-view shots came up. After a clip from the latter film, Ebert said:

Now that scene demonstrates a very common and probably very significant technique that's used again and again in these films. We view a scene through the eyes of the killer. You never saw the driver in that last scene. Instead, you saw everything though the driver's eyes. Now in the traditional horror movie, we often saw things from the victim's point of view but that's no longer. Now we look through the killer's eyes. It's almost as if the audience is being asked to identify with the attackers in these movies and that really bothers me.

Carol Clover, meanwhile, suggested the exact opposite in her groundbreaking book, *Men Women and Chainsaws: Gender in the Modern Horror Film* (1992), suggesting that the technique allowed male viewers to identify with the active female protagonist (or, as Clover dubs her in a phrase which has become common parlance, "the final girl"). A more prosaic explanation for the (over)use of the subjective camera is that it enables a director to hide the identity of the killer. In the extract singled out by Ebert, the driver is Mrs. Voorhees and framing the sequence "from the victim's point of view" would give away what should be the climactic big reveal. In what is perhaps the best-known example of the technique, the opening scene of *Halloween* (1978), John Carpenter's use of the device does enable us to "be" the killer stalking and gorily dispatching a topless young woman but it also serves to withhold the fact that the real killer is a child.

Girdler's film also seems to have had a marked influence on the British horror film, *Frightmare*. Pete Walker's film deals with a dysfunctional family in the heart of the English countryside ruled over by an elderly matriarch suffering from yet another "illness cannibalistic in nature" (screenwriter David McGillivray created the term, "cannibanthropy"). The central dynamic, weak but loving husband helping to harvest women for his wife to eat closely mirrors the earlier film. *Frightmare* was advertised with an ironic tagline lifted from the BBC Radio rural soap, *The Archers*, "an everyday story of country folk" and this could also be applied to *Meathook*. Girdler's film taps into a tradition of what's been dubbed "hixploitation", films that deal with the clash, sometimes violent, between city dwellers and country folk. *Deliverance* (1972) is probably the best-known example but H.G. Lewis's *Two Thousand Maniacs!*, with its Yankee tourists massacred by Southern rednecks, is also a key text. It's not solely a US tradition (*The Wicker Man* [1973] and the opening of *An American Werewolf in London* [1981] play on similar fears) but the ghosts of the Civil War lend an additional *frisson* to such conflicts. The violent Other in the form of savage country-dwellers would become more and more monstrous through the 70s, from the leering rapists of *Deliverance* to the mutant cannibals of *The Texas Chain Saw Massacre* to the even more mutated desert-dwelling family in *The Hills Have Eyes*. Pa may not be Leatherface but the journey from urban Louisville to rural Kentucky also ends up in murder, dismemberment and cannibalism.

Like *Asylum of Satan*, the film is visibly cheap with grainy cinematography (16mm blown up to 35), muffled sound and some amateurish performances. There's even one jarring moment where the screen goes black for no apparent reason. The budget was anywhere between $30,000 and $50,000 dollars, lower than his previous film, presumably due to the low returns on the debut feature. Girdler used left-over film stock from *Asylum* and his cast and crew were creatively resourceful, with actors wearing their own clothes as costumes. In the scene when Billy encounters the girls at night, the truck apparently broke down so crew members ended up pushing it into shot. There's some imaginative use of space and the farmhouse is an appropriately spooky setting. Pickett and Kissinger are both very good, the former very obviously channeling Anthony Perkins as the sensitive mother's boy, the latter alternating between taciturn and domineering with guests and icily reassuring with his son.

As noted, Sherry Steiner as Sherry is a vaguely alienating presence and she would go on to make appearances in a handful of 70s exploitation films, notably Larry Cohen's batshit *Demon* aka *God Told Me To* (1976). Madelyn Buzzard is also memorable as the unfortunate Becky. She would go on to play a small role (credited as "Whore") in Girdler's next film and then nothing aside from the lead in a late 90s short.

Unlike the frequently terse exchanges between Frank and Billy, the female characters are given some of the best, often florid lines. At the end of her first day on the farm, Sherry is rubbing her feet when she asks Becky:

Do you believe in reincarnation? I do. I know these feet have belonged to at least 3,000 people and now they're on their last legs.

In addition, her description of Louisville as a "concrete cage" seems to look forward to Girdler's next film, *The Zebra Killer*, with its scenes of urban mayhem. Becky gets one of the films weirdest moments, when she relates a heartfelt monologue about how she met her husband and how happy they were until:

They sent him an invitation to die in one of their wars. And they sent me a telegram that he had. But they were only half-right: I died too. Take all the happiness you can. At best, life's a short ride, and it isn't always round-trip.

It's an affecting scene, even if it does feel like it's from another film altogether and it's the kind of counterculture reference that turned up often in the horror films of the period. The social critiques in the work of Romero and Craven have been much discussed but 1972 also saw the release of *Deathdream* aka *Dead of Night*, Bob Clark's update of W. W Jacobs's *The Monkey's Paw* (1902) with a Vietnam vet coming home as a blood-drinking ghoul. *Deathdream* was written by Alan Ormsby, who would go on to write and co-direct (with Jeff Gillen) his own take on the Gein story, *Deranged*. The rest of the female cast are depicted less as individuals and more as a giggling bunch of free-spirited (ie. frequently nude) young women, the perfect victims for many a screen killer. It's notable that we don't actually hear their names until they're introduced to Pa at the farmhouse. The amount of (tan-lined) skin on show is another nod to the demands of the grindhouse crowd with all of the female performers (excepting the briefly-glimpsed Mama) being seen naked. The opening scene of Debbie (Linda Thompson) in bed is of extra note to Girdler obsessives because her lover is played by Hugh Smith. He would go on to be part of the crew on *The Zebra Killer* and *Abby* as well as playing a substantial role in the former film. He would go out to Los Angeles with the director but their relationship soured when, according to Smith, Girdler put his own name on a Smith screenplay, sold it and pocketed the cash. Smith went on to work on a handful of other exploitation films but reconciled with Girdler just weeks before that fateful helicopter crash:

Billy was a wonderful provider of opportunities and a sometime close friend. I still remember him with fondness and sadness. Those years when we all tried so hard to elevate ourselves into the rarified atmosphere of institutional Hollywood remain with me as a perpetual source of pride: Strange as it may seem to viewers of these awful movies we made (Smith in Breen 2000-1).

The director's score features some incongruous, vaguely inappropriate bits but this time it's used extremely effectively. The scene where Billy enters the house the morning after the massacre accompanied by a mournful harmonica and acoustic guitar lends real emotional power to what otherwise would have been another crowd-pleasing gore scene. There's also that jarring, discordant guitar to accompany the more suspenseful scenes. In another of the director's trademark touches, a lengthy musical interlude when Billy enters the club and he – and we – sit through a couple of songs by American Xpress, a band who must've seemed impossibly square in the early 70s. Some sample lyrics from their MOR protest song, "We're All Insane" include:

"Life is so ridiculous and I am so meticulous I don't even like black licorice and we're all insane.

Needles, pills, and sugarcubes and multi-colored neon tubes. People stuck in plastic groove and we're all insane".

As well as that wonderfully lurid title, one of the alternate taglines, "It's not one for the Bloody Mary at lunch bunch!" positions the film as defiantly lowbrow, in keeping with the new wave of grueling genre films which followed in the wake of the low-budget likes of *Night of the Living Dead* and the *Last House on the Left*. But in fact, it's fairly restrained by the standards of early 70s horror with the beheading and the pickaxe murder the stand-out shock moments. On reflection it isn't hard to see how the former effect was achieved, there's no Tom Savini-style effects wizardry going on but it's a startling image nevertheless. There's also a mounting intensity towards the end of the film, a kind of frenzy which can easily make a viewer forget just how comparatively sedate the previous hour was. Indeed, the pacing throughout is wildly out-of-kilter, the gruesome massacre near the start followed by the twin lulls of Billy's soul-searching and his putative courtship of Sherry. But the ending, from the sudden murder of Becky to the revelation that

Mama is alive just seconds before she gets a cleaver in the back rattles along at a breathless pace and provides a crowd-pleasing blend of blood, death and plot twists.

The trailer is eye-opening and in true exploitation style, more intense than the film itself. The gloomy, overwritten voiceover and visual restraint (with much of the trailer being the title in white on a black background) looks back to the ad campaign for *The Last House on the Left* ("To avoid fainting, keep repeating, 'it's only a movie'") and forward to the opening crawl of *The Texas Chain Saw Massacre*.

A picture you won't ever forget because it touches the full spectrum of the bizarre, the forbidden, the twilight areas of a life destined to be spent in shadow and agony. The screen may never again relate to this subject matter. It will certainly never again approach this treatment…Suspicion and fear, dwelling like a lodger in the mind, holding a black light to the dreams of childhood…a stolen life, pawn to a godless oblivion.

We get clips from the film, Billy and Pa arguing, stabbing, shooting and the flashback to Billy's childhood. We see Sherry opening the door to the smokehouse and seeing the hanging corpses, then it freezes on her terrified face and we hear her echoing scream. The voiceover gets even more hyberbolic.

The only ones left to mourn, the last witnesses to the execution, suspended in time by a puppeteer with blood on his hands, little broken dolls that go on a dancing after the music has stopped. Three on a Meathook.

In an episode of the webseries, *Trailers from Hell*, the director Eli Roth talks about Girdler's film and semi-seriously complains about the image from the smokehouse that gave the film its title, the women hanging in the barn: "It's not three on a meathook, it's three on three meathooks!"

Neither of Girdler's first features were financial hits but the director did right by his investors. He not only acknowledged them in print, telling *The Louisville Times* in 1977 how they "backed me when nobody else would. They made it possible for me to keep doing what I wanted to do. I was damned sure they'd get their money back someday" (Breen 2000-1), he went on to sign over the rights to both features. He didn't live to see the profits the films made on home video in the 1980s, their eye-catchingly lurid titles being exactly the kind of thing sensation-hungry renters were looking for. And with the desire for that elusive grindhouse thrill still strong for a certain kind of film freak, Girdler's second feature retains its lurid charms. For Darren Bauler, the programmer at the Spectacle in New York City, Girdler's low-budget frights are still big draws in what he refers to as "the midnight movie format":

"You get what you're looking for in a midnight movie," he says. "You can imagine it (as part) of a good double-feature in some rural drive-in somewhere." He says hyper-urbanized New York City residents are drawn in and creeped-out by the movie's slower, comparatively rural pace. "His early films really have that sense of place," he says. "And that's important to me." He also likes how the film seems to embody a sort of rough-around-the-edges feel, which puts it in contrast with slick Hollywood horror films. It makes it scarier (anon b. 2014).

On a visit to LA to screen *Meathook* as a showcase for his talents (and to show he could make features on ultra-low budgets), Girdler met David Sheldon and the two men would start a long and fruitful collaboration. Sheldon would go on to work on every remaining Girdler feature, either in a production capacity or writing, sometimes going uncredited.

I was the executive in charge of development at American International Pictures when Bill Girdler in Louisville frequently sent me stories and scripts to consider for production. None worked for me, but I was impressed with his creativity and persistence. He asked me if I would be interested in joining his newly formed Mid-American Pictures in Kentucky. I was looking for a way to leave AIP and start directing movies. I had directed over 100 plays and musicals in New York and at my summer theater, so I joined him as an equal partner. We agreed that we would alternate producing and directing. He would direct the first film and I would direct the 2nd, etc .

It isn't hard to see why the two of them got along so well, given that Sheldon's work up to that point anticipated what would become the Girdler *oeuvre*, from the eco-horror of *Frogs* (1972) to various Blaxploitation projects including the crime story *The Godfather of Harlem* (directed by cult auteur Larry Cohen) and *Blacula* (1972) and the sequel, *Scream Blacula Scream* (1973). He'd started his career at AIP and done some uncredited production work on *Black Mama, White Mama* (1973), a Pam Grier vehicle shot in the Philippines.

Sheldon produced the next Girdler film, which saw the director move away from horror without getting any more respectable. Indeed, unlike the oblique references to Ed Gein in his previous film, the director would reference a very recent string of murders to make his film appear a lot more topical than it actually was.

Chapter 4 - *The Zebra Killer* (1973): No Black Man Ever Killed Like This!!

AKA *Combat Cops, The Get-Man*.

Synopsis: The films begins with maverick cop Lt. Frank Savage (Austin Stoker) arriving at a horrendous crime scene, the gruesome murder of 3 nurses. Just how gruesome is related to us in seen-it-all cop-speak:

Two white females, one wrapped in a shower curtain lying on the bathroom floor stabbed six times in the body, got a colored female strangled with a stocking and her guts cut out, one lying on the bed, her throat slashed, lacerations on her back, looks like there was a possible rape. She looks like she probably bled out.

One nurse survives by hiding under a bed. The killer leaves a note at the scene, identifying himself as Mac and threatening thirteen more murders. As the investigation continues, he strikes again, planting a car bomb which kills a family of five. The surviving victim of the nurse massacre tells Savage that the killer was a black man with an afro. The next night, there's another victim, this time beaten to death with a sledgehammer and the following night, a hotel chambermaid is pushed down a flight of stairs. There are clues, including a black synthetic hair found at a crime scene and Frank works out that the victims, although chosen seemingly at random are being killed with the tools of their trade, the nurses with a scalpel, the chambermaid with a laundry basket. In his dilapidated hideout, Mac removes his wig and makeup to reveal he is, in fact, white (and played by the redoubtable James Pickett.) The next day he calls Savage and insinuates that they know each other. He also hands him a clue, "November 1971". The body count continues, with a man thrown down a lift shaft and although "Frank's Lady" is under police protection, Mac manages to kidnap her anyway (she's played by Valerie Rogers, whose character is unnamed throughout but she's credited as such). After trying to shoot Savage, Mac calls him and hands him one of those pointers that fictional bad guys like to hand out to their pursuers like breadcrumbs, that he's on his way to kill "the most important person next to you". He also gives him another date, 22nd April 1972. Savage finally comes up with a name and after calling the records department, we get footage of vintage computers and an exposition-heavy voiceover which explains that "Mac" stands for Milton Alexander Crowder. Sentenced in November 1971, he died in prison on the 22nd April. Furthermore, he had a young son with a criminal record and all of the murder victims were involved in Crowder's trial. Frank races to the house of the trial judge but Mac is already there. After some slightly implausible vacillating (although he'd already killed a lot of people without qualms), Mac shoots the judge and escapes, pursued by Frank. After a brief kung-fu bout (the inclusion of martial arts being another example of Girdler milking the *zeitgeist*), Frank is stabbed. He recovers quickly enough to kill a shooter, thinking he might be Mac (he isn't) before the man himself gets in touch, offering to trade Frank's Lady for a plane. Savage scuppers the plan, chases Mac back to his lair, shoots him dead (in crowd pleasing slow motion) and rescues his Lady.

Girdler's third feature was shot sometime in 1973 with even some of his close associates hazy about the details. The first Mid-America Pictures release (following the rebranding from Studio One), it was hastily put together and indeed, in many ways feels like a rush job. The director wrote the script with Gordon Cornell Layne (credited as Gordon C. Layne), a prolific composer, writer and producer. At the time of writing, he's still working 64 years after his first film as producer, *The Proud and Profane* (1956) and his credits include writing for the soap opera *Days of Our Lives* (1965 – date) and working as an associate producer on *Hart to Hart* (1979 – 96) and the 80s revival of *Alfred Hitchcock Presents* (1985). He was also an uncredited associate producer on the disaster movie *Airport* (1970).

In that aforementioned bit of opportunism, the original title references a sensational case of multiple murder in California which, though largely forgotten today, would've been a hot topic in 1974. The Death Angels, a Black Muslim gang based in San Francisco, killed 15 people in a string of racially motivated murders, although the number of victims may have been far higher (some sources suggest the group may have been responsible for 75 killings). The poster for the film's initial run suggests a clear connection, with an afro-sporting black man waving a machete and clutching a woman by the hair (one of the Zebra victims was a woman partially decapitated with a machete). However, Girdler just borrowed the title and the theme of racial violence while flipping it around, giving us a black cop hunting a white killer who poses as black. It's often described as a Blaxploitation film by people who haven't seen it but it's more accurately summed up as a Black *Dirty Harry*. In Don Siegel's landmark 1971 film, the title character, an unorthodox cop in a sports jacket hunts a psychotic racist kidnapper/killer in San Francisco while Girdler offers us an unorthodox cop in a sports jacket hunting a psychotic racist kidnapper/killer in Louisville. At several points, the later film uncannily mirrors its famous predecessor. Both start with murder and a note left by the killer and Girdler lifts a scene directly from the earlier film, with Savage finding a discarded shell casing on a roof top and picking it up with a pen. Harry's nemesis, Scorpio (a terrifying Andy Robinson) is a mixture of various American nightmares, a Charles Manson-style crazed hippy, a sniper who evokes the ghosts of Lee Harvey Oswald and James Earl Ray and a Zodiac Killer-style cop-taunting serial murderer. Indeed, according to David Sheldon, who started his long-time collaboration with the director on this film, Girdler originally wanted to have The Zodiac as Frank's nemesis but this was abandoned for fear of any legal complications that might ensue. Girdler, in true exploitation fashion, ups the ante considerably, referencing all manner of infamous crimes, both real and fictional, presenting Mac as a kind of walking, talking true crime compendium. His opening massacre of nurses is clearly inspired by the crimes of Richard Speck, even down to one of the victims surviving by hiding under a bed. The threatening notes and the use of different murder weapons smacks of the Zodiac and the film also taps into then-current anxieties about violent left-wing groups such as The Weather Underground and various black militant organizations, seemingly intent on indiscriminately planting bombs and killing cops. There are also nods to *Psycho* (one of the nurses is stabbed to death in the shower) and *Kiss of Death* (1947) with Mac recreating the shocking scene where Richard Widmark's giggling killer shoves a woman in a wheelchair down a flight of stairs, although this time it's a chambermaid in a laundry basket. Even the most incendiary aspect of Mac's crime spree (indeed, of the film itself), especially when seen today, the white killer blacking up and donning an afro wig to commit his crimes also has real-life parallels, with the Manson Family trying (ineptly as it happened) to shift the blame for their murders onto black militants or the British murderer and kidnapper, Donald Neilson aka the Black Panther adopting a fake West Indian accent while robbing sub-post offices.

Pickett is also tasked with outdoing Andy Robinson although this risks making Mac seem almost cartoonish in his villainy (something that never happens in Siegel's film, Scorpio always being shown as just human enough to be convincing). Mac's murderous minstrel show is presumably the aspect that led one reviewer to describe Girdler's film as "One of the most racist exploitation movies ever made" (Lew 2015), although this is a very simplistic reading. Mac is clearly exploiting the racist view of black people as criminals in order to evade capture. However, some of his lines are startling, such as the scene where he taunts the dead chambermaid with "you're an ugly nigger, you know that?" or Frank's Lady lying bound in bed and Mac with his face blacked referring to himself in the third person, musing, "If he hates niggers, how does he get all excited when he thinks about raping you?" Pickett's performance throughout is a thing of wonder, so over the top he's in orbit and displaying a remarkable array of sneers, threats and tics. The contrast between his Mac and the shy, troubled Billy in *Three on a Meathook* is a great illustration of his range as an actor.

A funnier, far gentler take on the issue of race can be seen in the relationship between Savage and his partner, Marty Williams (Hugh Smith) and the affectionate arguments they have on patrol. Savage asks Williams, "Are you saying we all look alike?" and is told, "Only at night". When Williams asks his partner why he smokes cheroots, Savage replies, "Because cigarettes are white". Similarly, there's one of those "only in the 70s" moments when Savage visits the sole survivor of the nurse massacre, an African-American woman, to "rap for a little while". She asks him, "Did they pick you because you're black?" and he replies, "No, baby, they picked me because I'm good."

The Savage/Williams black cop/white cop pairing would be given center stage in the ad campaign for the retitled version, *The Combat Cops* which, in an obvious attempt to cash in on the likes of *Freebie and the Bean* (1974) was repackaged as a buddy movie. The tag-line, 'Savage and Wilson are Combat Cops! A hard way to live! An easy way to die!' is notable partly because, presumably by accident, it renames Williams. There are some Blaxploitation touches scattered throughout the film, mostly centered on the flashily-dressed Pimp (D'Urville Martin), the band of unhappy prostitutes and the gangster character, the Big Man (who even gets his own theme song).

But Girdler's film fits more easily into the cycle of maverick cop films inspired not only by *Dirty Harry* but also the unconventional likes of *Bullitt* (1968), *Shaft* (1971) and *The French Connection* (1970). In this respect the visibly low-budget actually helps, making even the documentary-inflected realism of the latter film look polished in comparison. But alongside the faded colors and street scenes seemingly shot on the fly, there's a sloppiness with some scenes seemingly out of place and massive plot holes. The Big Man sub-plot goes nowhere and seems to exist primarily as the set-up to a weak visual gag, as the character is revealed to be a midget surrounded by massive henchmen. It's also unclear why he hands himself in to the police, although this is casually remarked upon later.

Despite the declaration in the end credits, "This motion picture is dedicated to the dedicated officers and men of the Louisville, Kentucky Police Department" the fact remains that Savage, as well as being a maverick, is also a lousy cop. His casual violence, disdain for authority and willingness to break the law are par for the course but too often he comes across as both slipshod and unhinged. After Mac taunts him in a phone call and boasts that he could "walk up to you in the street, man and ask you for a match and you still wouldn't know who I was", Frank attacks a black passerby who wants a light (*and* fails to apologize), despite the fact that he'd already guessed that Mac was in reality white. He also seems to go about his business even after finding out that his Lady is being held prisoner by a very prolific serial killer, going to karate practice and then on a drinking binge. It's not totally unfeasible that he would fail to remember the case of Milton Alexander Crowder, the executed father whose initials Mac uses for a name but the killer goes on to mention a couple of dates to Savage, when his father was convicted and when he was executed and he not only fails to remember but doesn't even bother to check the files. The fact that Mac hands his nemesis these key clues and Savage does nothing with them is indicative of his incompetence but also serves as a credibility-stretching plot hole, as does the fact that the killer's hideaway is in a building with "Mack" painted on the side in huge white letters. As Mac puts it as he rants to Frank's bound and gagged Lady, he "practically tells the police who he is". There are other inconsistencies and loose ends, some of which doubtless resulted from the quick turnaround (quick even for Girdler) and the film feels frequently disjointed and curiously unfinished. It's never made clear why Mac is out to get Savage, although we can surmise he was the cop who made the Crowder arrest and then there's the muddle surrounding the whole revenge scheme. Mac sets out to commit fourteen murders, indeed, there are so many some of them take place off-screen (we´re told that an air hostess was suffocated and a lawyer crushed by a bookcase). But he later states that Savage and the Judge will be his final victims, which means his body count stops at nine. Or are there other murders we – or Savage – don´t know about? It feels as if Girdler wasn´t overly interested in the script, a feeling that´s hard to shake with a few of these early films, regarding it simply as a way to string along a series of action sequences and murders. The filmmaker and critic Douglas Buck has written of his love for Girdler, describing him as a "died-tragically.and-way-too-young 70´s indie drive-in style filmmaker" (Buck 2017) but he also can see the problems with *The Zebra Killer*:

It´s more than likely these narrative/character problems came from those familiar uber low budget short schedules that allowed little in the way of anything other than shooting what they could rather than what they needed but, where in certain cases that quick decision-making ends up being a strength and/or charm of the film, in this case it unfortunately hampers the narrative (Buck 2017).

For Steve Puchalski, the ineptitude of both the protagonist and the script is part of the appeal for the "undoubtedly drunk or stoned" audience who will doubtless get off on the "laughable accidental carnage, since every time Savage barely escapes death, some unlucky bystander gets offed instead" (Puchalski 2000).

Glaring script issues aside, the film benefits considerably from the unfamiliar settings and there´s lots of footage of an eerily underpopulated city at night. A number of landmarks make an appearance, including the steamboat Belle of Louisville which figures prominently in the scene where Mac flees from the security guard. In one shot, underlining Girdler´s status as a hometown boy, we even get a glimpse of a cinema billboard advertising *Three on a Meathook*. There´s also a number of interesting supporting characters, from the casually racist, cigar-smoking female newspaper seller/porn dealer who doubles up as Frank´s informer (who tells him, in another of those only-in-the-70s lines, "you may be black but you ain't stupid") to "the sloppy seven", a bunch of raucous streetwalkers dressed somewhat incongruously in evening gowns who Frank catches beating up their pimp with sticks. There are a couple of effective scenes which stand out, especially the Hitchcockian sadism as Mac stalks his second victim. He watches the man through a sniper sight but contrary to our expectations, fails to shoot. When the man, along with wife and kids gets into the car, there's a tense moment when he turns the key in the ignition but again, nothing happens save for the car starting. It's a case of third time unlucky as the driver finds a parcel in the car, which suddenly explodes, killing them all. It's not only a well-done bit of suspense but also a very 70s bit of paranoia, the sense that danger can strike anytime in any form in this violent, turbulent decade. There are a couple of the director's usual touches, a couple of easy listening soul songs which accompany key scenes and there's also quite a few familiar faces from the Girdler stock company. Pickett, of course and Girdler staple Charles Kissinger, this time round giving an impressively naturalistic performance as a cop. There's also an appearance by Madelyn Buzzard, one of the victims in *Meathook* and a blink-and-you'll-miss-her cameo from Carla Rueckert as a murdered nurse. Austin Stoker would go on to make a couple more films with Girdler before his signature role in John Carpenter's *Assault on Precinct 13* (1976) while D'Urville Martin would return for *Sheba Baby* (the suit he's wearing here turns up in that film worn by another actor). The veteran Juanita Moore, whose credits included *Imitation of Life* (1959) and a handful of influential Blaxploitation pictures including *The Mack* (1973) and *Thomasine and Bushrod* (1974) would also play a substantial role in *Abby*. The real surprise here is Hugh Smith as Frank's partner, Marty Williams, a sardonic yet loyal sidekick and good enough to make one wish he'd acted more. In an uncredited role, Mike Clifford appears as a cop called Waldo. He was a homicide detective turned technical adviser and part of his job was to act as an intermediary between Girdler and the Louisville police, giving the filmmakers access to squad cars and real cops as extras. Like many other collaborators, Clifford would go on to become a member of the Girdler crew, working in a variety of roles (transportation chief on *Day of the Animals*, location manager on *Grizzly* and small acting roles in both pictures).

The release of *The Zebra Killer* was patchy and inconsistent, something that would happen to a couple of other Girdler films. It had some limited screenings in the US, sometimes playing as *The Get-Man Against the Zebra Killer* and a wider release in Europe retitled *Panic City* and *Combat Cops*. It´s far from the director´s best but there´s considerable appeal in its sleazy, fast-paced charms:

Yes, it´s unsubtle, under-financed rotgut, which looks like shit and blows its wad early on, before degenerating into a standard chase; but its ballsy, anything-goes sensibilities continually makes up for any shortcomings (Puchalski 2000).

The Hidan of Maukbeiangjow: **If You Can´t Say It, Go See it!**

This oddball slice of science-fiction comedy merits a mention here as it features so many Girdler alumni. The ominous opening sequence of a van pulling up outside an isolated farmhouse and two men carrying a bound and masked woman inside suggests a dark thriller, an impression immediately undercut by the truly terrible song which plays over the credits, a corny slice of *faux* country and western that makes even the insipid musical interludes in Girdler movies sound great. The lyrics to this opening number can be read as an ironic comment on the almost incomprehensible, borderline unwatchable thing we´re about to watch, "If you think you understand what´s going on, my friend, I can tell you for sure that you´re wrong". It´s the story of a private eye teaming up with some hippies to bust a kidnapping ring abducting young women for a cult, who then kill them and resurrect them as zombies. Early on, the PI gets his instructions on a cassette tape, *Mission Impossible*-style and the fact that the tape eventually self-destructs in someone´s back pocket is a level of the kind of humor on show.

Studio One provided the equipment for the shoot and the end result does resemble a Girdler film in some ways, being visibly underfunded and featuring not only some familiar faces but also some familiar locations (the farmhouse from *Meathook*, for example). The director Lee Jones worked in various capacities on Girdler's first two features and would return for *Grizzly* (he even pops up in that film as "Man being interviewed"). He was also an associate of JG Patterson. Hugh Smith appears as the "private pig" leading the investigation and Carla Rueckert, in dark glasses and what looks to be a wig, plays one of the kidnap victims, a role intended for another actor who refused at the last minute to perform the topless scenes demanded by distributors (the fact that she's topless for the majority of her screen time might have been what swayed the original candidate). Rueckert's husband at the time, James De Witt is the guilty party behind the truly terrible songs.

Screenwriter/producer/assistant director Phineas T. Pinkham was, in reality, Don Elkins and while this, his sole feature as writer/producer is a comedy, he took his Ufology very seriously indeed. His other credits bear this obsession out, appearing as an interviewee on a TV show about flying saucers and popping up in the documentary, *The Force Beyond* (1977), a sub-Erich von Däniken alien spaceman opus from the director of *The Incredible Melting Man* (1977). Elkins, Rueckert and her second husband Jim McCarty founded L/L Research based in Louisville which describes itself as "a non-profit organization dedicated to discovering and sharing information to aid in the spiritual evolution of mankind". *The Hidan of Maukbeiangjow* is ultimately every bit as bad as that title suggests, a mélange of silly fight scenes, poor gags and half-baked new age psychobabble. For obvious reasons, it was eventually retitled but even renamed *Invasion of the Girl Snatchers*, it failed to find an audience. In the 1980s, it acquired a cult following among Bad Movie afficionados, in part due to a tagline which was better than the film, "Earth's Hippies against Zombies from Outer Space!" (just where would exploitation taglines be without exclamation marks?). As with *Dr. Gore*, sitting through *The Hidan of Maukbeiangjo* would make most if not all Girdler agnostics reappraise their position. It's not that it's inept (although it is) and muddled (ditto), it's more that for a supposed comedy, it's painfully unfunny.

And Girdler? His Louisville films had served as an effective calling card for Hollywood and it made sense that he would end up at American International Pictures. Started in 1954 by James H. Nicholson and Samuel Z. Arkoff, AIP set out to produce low-budget exploitation films aimed at a teenage crowd and this led to their impressive track record for attracting and nurturing young talent. On a TV talk show in the 1980s, Arkoff explained the company's formula for success, a formula which bore his name:

Action (exciting, entertaining drama)
Revolution (novel or controversial themes and ideas)
Killing (a modicum of violence)
Oratory (notable dialogue and speeches)
Fantasy (acted-out fantasies common to the audience)
Fornication (sex appeal for young adults)

This formula meant they could rework their product to appeal to a constantly changing teenage demographic. So the drag racing and rock and roll films of the late 1950s (*Dragstrip Girl* [1957] and *Rock All Night* [1957] begat the beach party movies of the early 60s [*Summer Holiday* [1964], *Muscle Beach Party* [1964]) which begat the biker and acid movies aimed at the late 60s turned on crowd (*The Wild Angels* [1967], *The Trip* [1967]). By 1970, they may have lost their best-known talent, producer/director Roger Corman but AIP was still a hugely profitable enterprise. Their *modus operandi* of churning out low-budget variations on big studio hits suited Girdler, who'd been doing a similar thing from his Kentucky base and as both producers and distributors, they were also drawn to horror, crime and science fiction, lurid fare which appealed to a young, hip crowd. Indeed, a look at the early 70s AIP catalogue is an insight into what today looks like a Golden Age of Exploitation, running the gamut from British gothic (*The Vampire Lovers* [1970]), *The Abominable Dr. Phibes* [1970]), *gialli* [*Lizard in a Woman's Skin* [1971]) and biker movies [*Chrome and Hot Leather* [1971]) to groovy satire [*Gas-s-s-s* [1970], sexploitation (*Together* [1972]) and even the odd way-out documentary (the Oscar-nominated *Manson* [1973]). *Abby* was a perfect fit for AIP, offering a blend of two such popular exploitation strands, horror and Blaxploitation, a synthesis that, according to the director, came about after seeing just how many people waiting on line for *The Exorcist* were African-American (see cultfilmalley 2020). It's certainly true that Friedkin's film was popular with black audiences, as noted in a New York Times article from 1974 headlined, "They Wait Hours to be Shocked":

Anywhere from a fourth to a third of the crowd was black, generally a high figure for an East Side theater. One black Manhattan secretary explained it to me this way: "A lot of blacks relate to voodoo and witchcraft and that kind of devil stuff. Many still believe in black magic, especially those from Haiti and the Deep South." (Klemesrud 1974).

But this combination wasn't exactly a new one, what with the likes of *Blacula* and its sequel, *Scream, Blacula, Scream*, films which *Abby* producer and long-time Girdler collaborator David Sheldon had worked on. However, whereas *Blacula* imaginatively reworked decades of screen vampire lore, *Abby* would owe a bit too much to that recent box-office smash. The author Jim Knipfel has written about the change in the director's thinking that occurred leading up to his first AIP film:

In extremely low-budget terms, Girdler, it must be said, started out with a good deal of energy and some promise. He was even a little ahead of the curve. Just a smidgen. Problem is, if you're only ten minutes ahead of your time, you're pretty well screwed (Knipfel 2016).

For Knipfel, *Asylum of Satan* anticipated the satanic cycle made big by *The Exorcist* and *Meathook* was first in the mini-wave of

Gein-inspired slasher movie but both films arrived just a bit too early to be hits:

It seems around that same point [1973] he realized there was much more money to be made in being ten minutes behind the times than there was in being ten minutes ahead of them. I mean, why bother putting all that work into making (mostly) original movies with a unique angle when you could just spit out a cheap remake of a proven hit? (Knipfel 2016).

Although he´s writing about *Abby*, *The Zebra Killer* and its liberal (pardon the pun) borrowings from *Dirty Harry* can also be regarded as "a cheap remake of a proven hit". From this point on, Girdler would specialize in making homages to/rip-offs of commercial hits. And none would be as controversial as *Abby*.

Chapter 5 - *Abby* (1974): Abby Doesn´t Need a Man Anymore... The Devil is her Lover Now!

Synopsis: The film opens with a low-key farewell picnic for Doctor Garret Williams (William Marshall) arranged by his students. Somewhat ominously, Williams, a doctor and bishop, mentions his plan to visit a cave in Nigeria where a cult used to practice their rites. The cult was devoted to the African demon, Eshu and would "rejoice in evil and violent acts". His going away present is a large cross necklace. In Nigeria, Williams finds a carved box in a cave, decorated with a likeness of Eshu, with cox comb and "erect penis". When the box is opened, the dust inside is blown away and a howling wind starts up in the cave, which appears to kill Williams´s two guides. There is also a flash edit of a green female monster, although it appears long enough for us to see it´s essentially a Halloween mask, unlike the unnerving flickering demon face in *The Exorcist*.

Meanwhile Williams´s son, Emmett (Terry Carter), also a preacher, is in the process of moving into a large house in Louisville which has been bequeathed to the church. Emmett is married to Abby (Carol Speed), whose goodness is underlined with some pointed expository dialogue, as when her mother (Juanita Moore) hears the news that her daughter´s qualified as a marriage counselor: "Oh really? On top of the youth program and working with the junior choir?" Her mother and cop brother, Cass (Austin Stoker, fresh from *The Zebra Killer*) are also on hand to help the couple settle in. This seemingly idyllic homely setting is undercut that first night, with howling wind, shaking furniture and slamming doors. The next morning, Abby masturbates in the shower (something we´re clearly supposed to regard as, if not bad then at the very least out of character) and in the cellar, there´s a supernatural wind and another appearance by that green-faced demon. When Abby´s cutting up some bleeding chicken, she has a funny turn, flicking her tongue in and out in a manner which is both vaguely lascivious and disturbing before she gashes her own arm. The next day, Abby is singing in the church choir when she starts to choke and retch before vomiting on an unfortunate churchgoer. Later, when Emmett plays seducer, approaching the marital bed half-naked and quoting the Song of Solomon (!), Abby kicks him in the groin and shouts in a voice which isn´t hers. Emmett and Cass try to find a rational solution for Abby´s ills, such as childhood trauma or drug use but she becomes increasingly unpredictable, gatecrashing the preacher´s marriage guidance session and making a crude come-on to the husband. There´s a wry joke in Emmett´s response, "Whatever possessed you to do a thing like that?" When Abby is visited by a concerned parishioner, she ends up abusing the poor woman in that demon voice before all hell breaks loose (pardon the pun), with furniture shaking and flying through the air and the TV exploding. Abby starts foaming at the mouth and the unfortunate visitor has a heart attack. Emmett consults a doctor (played by Girdler regular Charles Kissinger) before calling his father in Nigeria, telling him how his wife "may have killed someone". In another scene transplanted from *The Exorcist*, Abby goes to the hospital for tests but they can find nothing wrong with her. In her room, she is again transformed and tells Emmett how she´s waiting for his "motherfucking father". She then goes on to cause chaos, attacking patients before storming out. When Emmett arrives home, accompanied by Garrett, Abby is back to her cheery self, almost eerily calm and polite. She makes a pass at the bishop and when he rejects her, she again gets violent. She leaves the house and although Emmett hijacks a passing car to try and catch her, she escapes into night-time Louisville. There follows the by-now familiar footage of the city as Emmett searches the streets and bars. In one eerie scene, he stops at a telephone box and the phone starts ringing, the demon is on the line. Back at the house, Garrett explains the situation to Cass, telling him how "Quite unintentionally I released the spirit of

Eshu while I was in Africa and as part of his campaign to destroy me he now has control over your sister". Back downtown, Abby attempts to seduce a funeral director and fellow churchgoer before molesting him in a non-specific fashion in his car, the vehicle rocking up and down and belching smoke. A soul song (in actuality, the theme song sung by Speed) accompanies Emmett and Cass's search for Abby while back at the house, Garrett finds "help me" scrawled on a mirror in lipstick. When Emmett finally catches up with Abby, who is doing some serious flirting with a couple of bar patrons, she encourages them to humiliate him, initiating a game of "Strip the Preacher". The whole crowd seems to join in until Cass fires a couple of shots into the ceiling to disperse them. After she beats up Cass and Emmett, Abby turns her violence on the men she was drinking with, sending one sliding the length of the bar in a manner more silly than scary. Garrett arrives and Abby runs from the sight of the cross he wears, her movements slowed-down and the soundtrack composed of amplified moans and echoing howls. The exorcism taking place in a wrecked disco is a novel touch, as is the bishop donning traditional African dress, the suggestion being that ultimately Yoruba magic is stronger than traditional Christianity. Girdler does his best to jazz up the exorcism scene, with rapid cuts and destruction of property as well as a lot of colored gels. The demonic dust slowly goes back into the box it came from and Abby is left, her face burned and smoking. In a very brief tacked-on scene we see Emmett and his now demon-free wife bidding farewell to family members as they board a plane. It really feels as if the minute the thrills and action are done, Girdler is keen to wrap things up as quickly as possible.

It's impossible to talk about *Abby* without mentioning *The Exorcist*. After all, the plentiful borrowing from Friedkin's enormously profitable film wasn't exactly a secret. As the director himself admitted, with disarming, possibly unwise, honesty,"Sure, we made 'Abby' to come in on the shirttail of 'The Exorcist.'" (in Breen 2000-1). According to J. Patrick Kelly, who this time round worked as Production Manager, the crew "lived in fear" of getting sued (Ibid.). Only a couple of years later, Girdler would recycle the elements of *Jaws* and score the biggest hit of his career with *Grizzly* but his extended homage to/rip-off of Friedkin's film landed him in court.

One of the reasons *Abby* became a target for the lawyers was its massive commercial success, the picture earning more than half a million dollars in its first five days of release. AIP took out ad describing the film as "a Christmas present for Mr. Exhibitor!" and listing just how much the film took in in different cities, $83,733 in one NYC theater, $30,027 in another and more than $80,000 in Chicago. Estimates suggest that it ended up taking in over $4,000,000 (on a $200,000 budget!) But four weeks into its run, Warner Brothers filed a lawsuit against Girdler and AIP alleging copyright infringement, the profits were frozen and the film was withdrawn. Then things get murky, as various sources tell different versions of what happened and to this day, *Abby*'s status in unclear. A settlement in 1978 saw AIP getting their money back but the film still seems to be in limbo, with a copy posted on YouTube and three different DVD releases in 2006-7. All of these copies seem to have been sourced from a 16mm print which isn't in the best shape, with washed-out colors and scratches but no-one seems to know what happened to the original raw materials or indeed, whether the Warner injunctions still stands. Mark Hasan has dubbed it "the most widely-seen corporate suppressed blaxploitation film in history" (Hasan 2017) while also pointing out that there's more to the story than just the lawsuit, noting how the Italian Exorcist-rip-off *Beyond the Door/ Chi Sei?* (1974) was also the target of Warner's ire and yet that film's been available in various forms for a long time (see Hasan 2017). This is an occupational hazard in the low-budget exploitation field, wrangles over rights, distribution woes and missing film elements and it's surely one of the reasons why Girdler's films have frequently been so poorly served, with shoddy prints, grey market releases and some sketchy distribution (the fact that no-one seems to be entirely clear about *The Zebra Killer*'s release history is just one example).

One odd footnote to the lawsuit is the input of William Peter Blatty, author of the source novel and the screenplay for *The Exorcist*. According to Jerry Veneman, writing in 2002:

William Peter Blatty, author of the novel *The Exorcist*, was against the lawsuit. In one interview, Blatty said, "I visited the set of *Abby*. Director William Girdler was just trying to make a different version of *The Exorcist* and I had no problem with that. I actually liked *Abby*." He refused to act against *Abby* when Warner sued and, to this day, still disagrees with the action (2002).

Blatty may have disagreed with the lawsuit but it´s hard to imagine anyone involved with Girdler´s film forgetting to mention his visit to the set, especially given the aforementioned concerns about being sued. Surely someone would see Blatty´s approval as an important endorsement? The interview with Blatty isn´t referenced but Pat Kelly is understandably dubious, "If William Blatty visited the set of *Abby*, it was undercover…I think it would be more than a rumor if he had been there" (in Breen 2000-1).

While *Abby* adheres closely to the Friedkin template (with Marshall even being given some of Max Von Sydow´s lines *verbatim* in the exorcism sequence), it differs in some important respects. One of the most striking things about *The Exorcist* was the state-of-the-art effects, the levitating Regan, bouncing beds, a head turned 360 degrees and the justly famous projectile vomiting. There was no way, with such a small budget and limited resources, that Girdler could compete (at $12 million dollars, the budget for *The Exorcist* was 120 times that of *Abby*). But necessity being the mother of invention, Girdler and his crew found some low-tech ways to depict *Abby*´s plight. White foam replaces the pea soup vomit, there´s a message scrawled on lipstick on a mirror rather than the words etched in skin and according to David Sheldon, the shaking room effects were achieved by placing hand vibrators on either side of the camera.

The demon voice was provided by Bob Holt, an actor best-know for voicing characters in dozens of cartoons including *The Lorax*

(1972) and *The Nine Lives of Fritz the Cat* (1974) (in the latter film one of the characters he plays is God). His work as Eshu, complete with a lot of echo is effective enough but it's no match for the chilling job Mercedes McCambridge did in Friedkin's film. Another important element which contributed both to the box-office success and the notoriety of *The Exorcist* is the shock factor. The language and the sexualized situations that Regan finds herself in, be it genital mutilation by crucifix or shoving her bloody crotch into her mother's face, still retain the power to shock decades later. Traditionally, one of the draws of the low-budget independents has been shock value, whether it be the gore of *Blood Feast* and *Night of the Living Dead*, the unsimulated sex of *Deep Throat* (1972) or the unsimulated coprophilia of *Pink Flamingoes* (1973) but in this respect *Abby* is positively coy. This is typical for a director who, for all his exploitation credentials, was often reticent to go too far when it came to sex and violence. There's undoubtedly a lot of potential for lurid thrills in Girdler's films, be it satanism, cannibalism or racist serial killers but he generally tended to avoid too much graphic nastiness. That disturbing element is further reduced by making the victim a grown woman rather than a child. A good example of this reticence is when Abby masturbates in the shower. I've written elsewhere how female masturbation is often used by genre filmmakers as a device to suggest instability (see Cooper 2016). Compare this depiction of what is, by any sane measure, totally normal behavior (even for a preacher's wife) with the masturbation/ genital mutilation scene in Friedkin's film which manages to be violent, blasphemous and far more disturbing given that Regan is only 12. *The Exorcist* also benefits considerably from the clash between the deeply-held spiritual beliefs of screenwriter Blatty and Friedkin's icy misanthropy whereas Girdler evidently isn't really sold on the religious aspects and his vision of the world is much less harsh.

As Abby, Carol Speed is more convincing as a marriage guidance counselor and preacher's wife than she is a woman inhabited by an

African demon. The scenes where she's asked to perform lecherously, be it solo in the shower or later in the bars and discos of Louisville are pretty unconvincing, in the latter scenes she comes over more drunk than evil. There are some tantalizing subversive racial politics at play, although Girdler doesn't really develop them. As Kim Newman puts it:

Pre-possession, Abby dresses all in white and acts so respectably that radical African-Americans might accuse her of selling out to White Amerikka (her cake-baking mother is even played by Juanita Moore, the archetypal self-sacrificing housekeeper from *Imitation of Life*). When an *African* spirit takes up residence, the soul sister becomes a gross racial caricature – wild-haired, foul-mouthed, promiscuous, violent, but also sexy, self-assured, stylish and (crucially for the genre) jive-talking (Newman 2022).

Although Speed plays the title character, the real draw is William Marshall. Standing 6'5" tall and with a sonorous voice, he had an impressive theatrical career encompassing Shakespeare and opera but his charismatic, imposing manner may have held back his screen career somewhat. He was clearly a leading man and most roles for African-American actors in the 1950s and early 1960s were supporting parts. His career also suffered setbacks as a result of his left-wing politics, as when *Harlem Detective* (1953), a TV show he had a major role in, was cancelled after a newspaper article described Marshall as a communist. He did appear in shows including *Bonanza* (1959 – 73) and *Star Trek* (1966 – 9) and films including *The Boston Strangler* (1968), which also starred the future star of *The Manitou*, Tony Curtis. His signature role was as the eponymous vampire in *Blacula* and its sequel *Scream Blacula Scream*. Despite the gimmicky titles, they're excellent examples of Blaxploitation horror and along with the *Count Yorga* films (1970 – 1), fascinating in the way they update some hoary gothic horror conventions for the hip and cynical 70s. Marshall takes the role of undead African Prince completely seriously and a large part of the film's appeal comes from his brand of doomy romanticism. Although he's very good as Reverend

Williams, he was reportedly unhappy with *Abby*. Some of his lines in the exorcism sequence were reportedly written by the actor and he also apparently knew a lot more about Yoruba than Girdler or Layne did. As the New York Times put it, "Mr. Marshall does manage to be dignified despite the mumbo-jumbo he's involved with" (anon c. 1974). The film also showcases a number of members of the Girdler stock company, from Austin Stoker and Juanita Moore to Claude Fulkerson, appearing in a weird cameo as a lounge lizard trying to impress the demonic Abby.

Taken on its own merits, *Abby* is a strange film, the first half being an atmospheric horror tale, the second half slowing dramatically before fizzling out. The house inherited by Abby and Emmett is a very spooky location, rambling and bare, often shot at night through mist. The scene where Abby interrupts her marriage guidance session by tearing her shirt open and threatening to take the nonplussed husband upstairs to "fuck the shit out of him" is clearly intended to be a crowd-pleasing moment, as funny as it is awkward but there are more subtle scares in the house. The moment when a shadow can be glimpsed on the curtain approaching Abby as she showers is a subtle visual indicator of possession, as well as being a nod to Hitchcock. But the film goes off the rails when Abby escapes and goes bar hopping, violently attempting to seduce a church parishioner, flirting and drinking. The seemingly endless scenes in these establishments are of some sociological interest (were the bars at that time really so brightly-lit or was it just for the filming? What's with all that orange?), showcasing the dancing and often outlandish headwear of the nightclub crowd of the period. This material also serves to showcase the director's love of music and his habit of taking time out from the plot to play a song or two. Indeed, this devotion to the groove is summed up in a lengthy shot of a record being lined up to play in a jukebox. But that aside, any tension the film built up is fatally dissipated. Whereas in Friedkin's film the scale of the action shrinks throughout, from an Iraqi archaeological dig and a Hollywood film shoot to the actual exorcism which takes place in one small bedroom, here the action is opened out, from the house to a succession of night spots. The exorcism takes place in an empty bar and while there is some striking imagery (a flaming mirror ball and some rapidly edited scenes of destruction), Girdler doesn't come close to recapturing the uneasy atmosphere of the earlier film. It wouldn't be a 70s occult horror outing if there weren't some allegations of supernatural activity (as is the case with both *The Exorcist* and *The Omen* [1978]). Speed has talked about people falling ill and the tornadoes that hit Kentucky during the filming but as J. Patrick Kelly notes, those tornadoes also hit nine other states (in Breen 2000-1), states where they weren't filming *Abby*. But in Girdler's next film, *Sheba Baby*, also shot in Louisville, these same tornadoes get a mention, they were clearly big news in Kentucky.

It's tempting to wonder if anyone came to *Abby* without having seen *The Exorcist* and just how potent some of Girdler's imagery would be, in that case. As it is, the diabolical goings on can't help but feel like a decaffeinated take on the earlier film. There's also a marked contrast in the way both films were marketed. The subtle, almost cryptic poster design for the Friedkin film featured a still image of Von Sydow's Merrin standing outside the McNeill house in a shaft of light, giving no hint of the lurid excesses which awaited theatergoers. But *Abby* is keen to emphasize its thrills, most of the poster images and adverts featuring Speed in her demon make-up, usually with a background of hellish flames and the unambiguous tagline, "Abby doesn't need a man anymore, the devil is her lover now".

There's also something ironic about an African-American take on *The Exorcist*, given that Friedkin's film is cited as a factor in the demise of the Blaxploitation cycle. As Maitland McDonagh put it:

Studio executives took note of the fact that a substantial piece of the box office for films like *The Godfather* (1972) and *The Exorcist* (1973) was generated in black communities and concluded that they could get black people into theatres without having to make specifically black-oriented films (McDonagh 2004:118).

Ultimately, it's a pity that *Abby* is so often dismissed as nothing more than a cheap clone as it's an important slice of black horror. This latter aspect has taken on additional importance in recent years with a growing awareness of, as the title of a feature documentary on the subject puts it, *Horror Noire* (2019). This emphasis has sprung up partly in the wake of Jordan Peele's *Get Out* (2017) and has seen renewed attention placed on cult oddities such as Bill Gunn's *Ganja and Hess* (1973), remade by Spike Lee as *Da Sweet Blood of Jesus* (2014). It's hard to see a similar cult springing up around Girdler's film any time soon. Like a lot of Blaxploitation entries, it was made by a white director and its reputation as a shameless rip-off has sadly made it more notorious than celebrated. But it has a lingering afterlife as a jokey reference in the scattershot Blaxploitation parody, *I'm Gonna Get You Sucka* (1988). A stressed waitress turns demonic when approached in the street – with wild hair, white eyes and a deep voice – but the cause is not Satan but menstrual cramps.

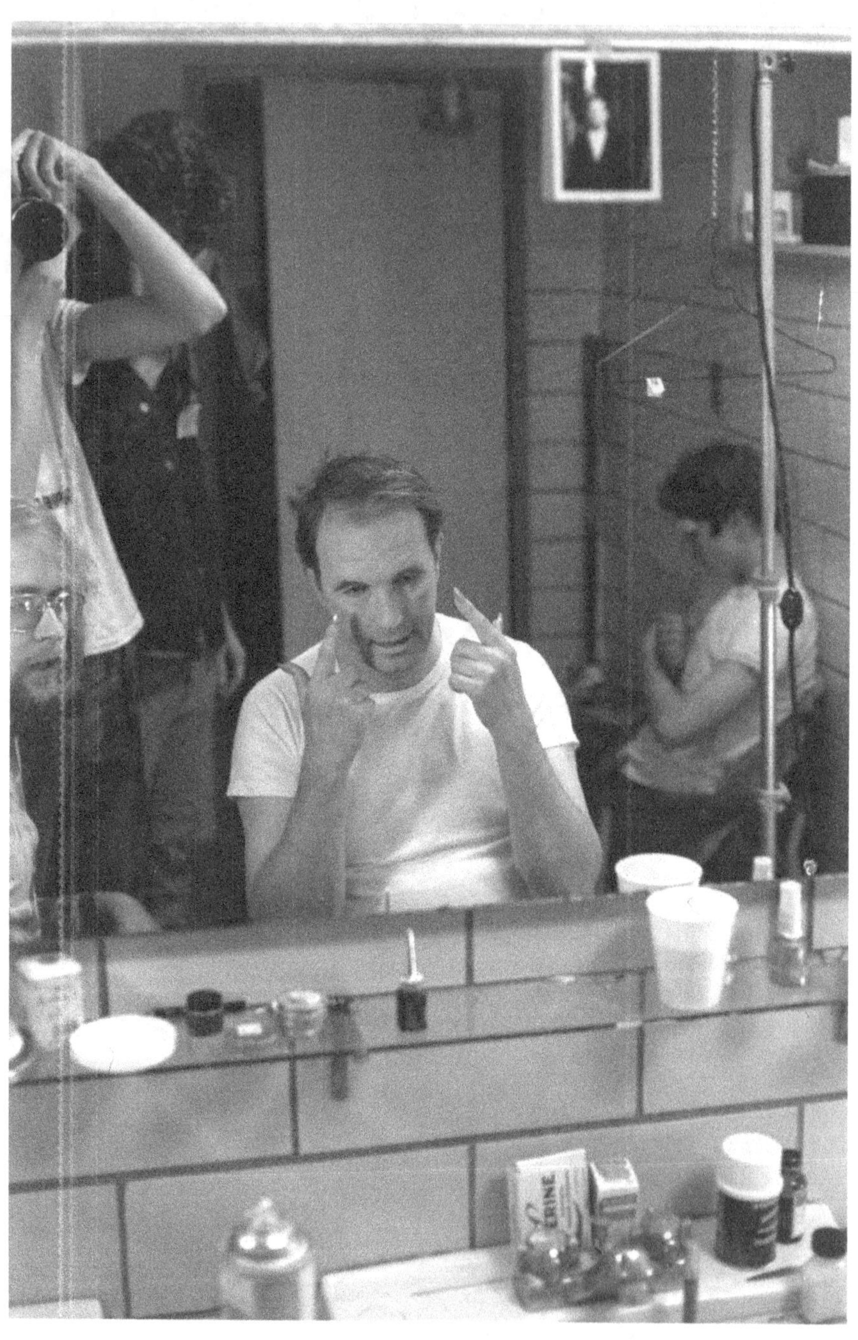

Charles Kissinger behind the scenes on Asylum of Satan (photograph © Don Wrege 2022)

William Girdler on the set of Asylum of Satan (photograph © Don Wrege 2022)

Lt. Walsh (Louis Bandy) and Chris (Nick Jolley) in Asylum of Satan (photograph © Don Wrege 2022)

Carla Borelli behind the scenes on Asylum of Satan (photograph © Don Wrege 2022)

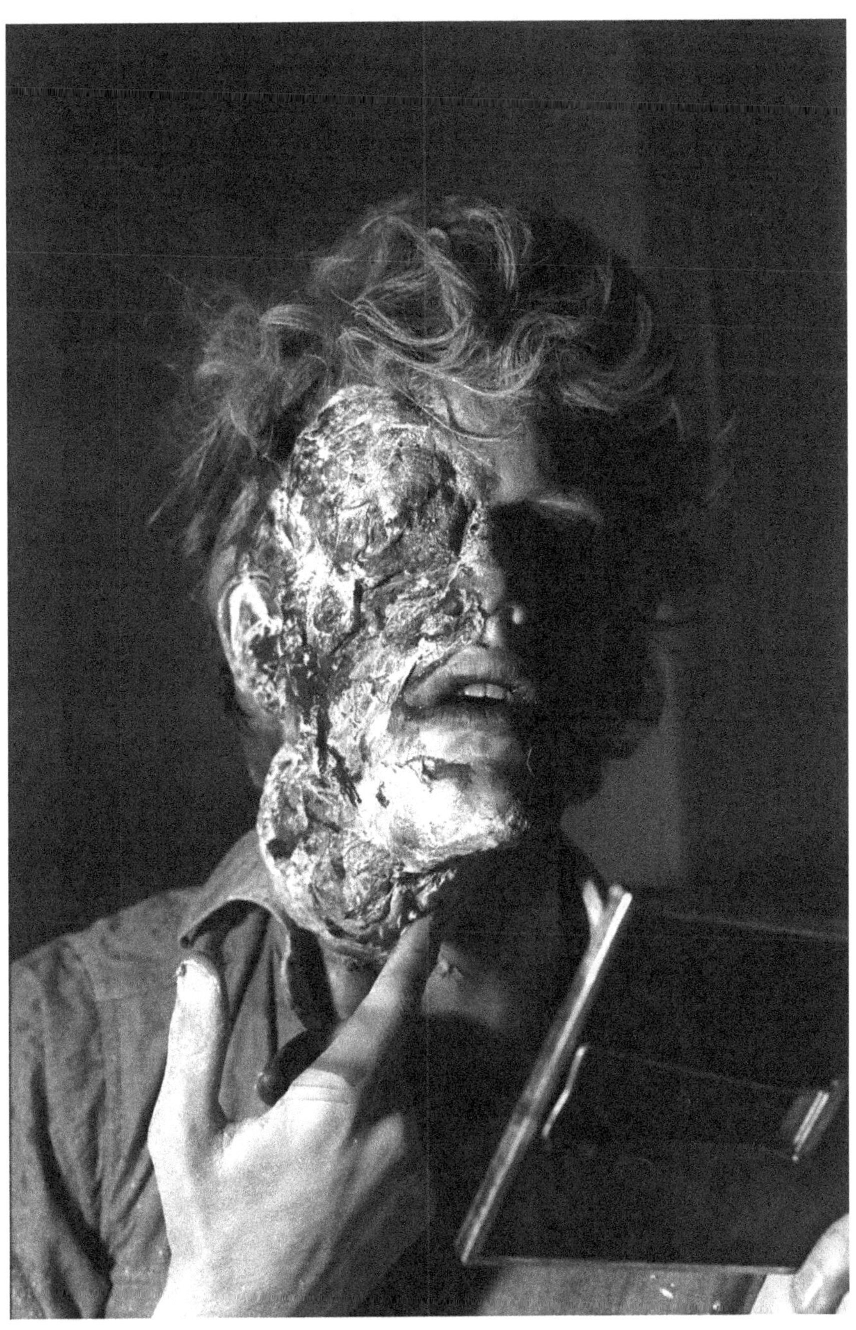

James Pickett in Asylum of Satan (photograph © Don Wrege 2022)

Carla Borelli behind the scenes on Asylum of Satan (photograph © Don Wrege 2022)

Louisville´s own Claude Fulkerson in Asylum of Satan (photograph
© Don Wrege 2022)

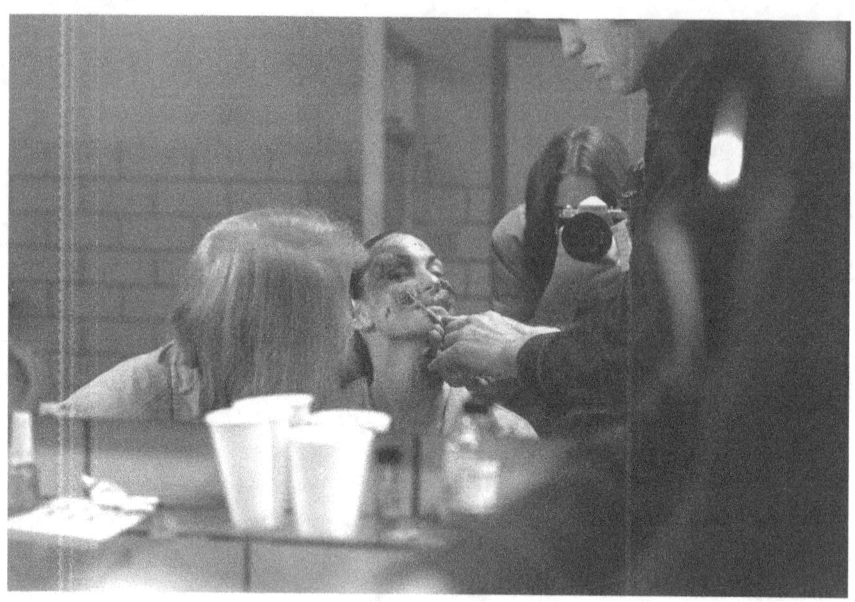

Sherry Steiner being made up under the watchful lens of set photographer
Don Wrege on Asylum of Satan (photograph © Don Wrege 2022)

The unconvincing devil mask from Asylum of Satan.

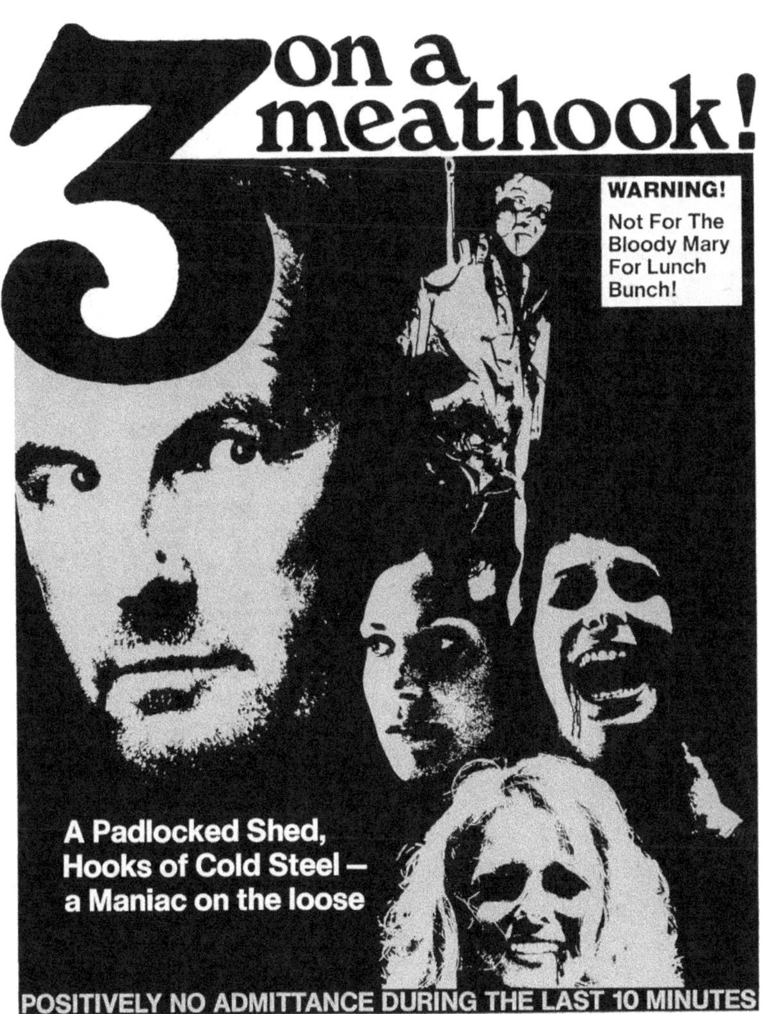

A characteristically lurid poster for Three on a Meathook.

Frank and his pickaxe in Three on a Meathook.

One of the many posters for The Zebra Killer.

the ZEBRA KILLER
HAS THE CITY IN PANIC
"NO BLACK MAN EVER KILLED LIKE THIS!!"
ARTHUR MARKS PRESENTS
the ZEBRA KILLER
COLOR
starring AUSTIN STOKER — JAMES PICKETT — HUGH SMITH
co-starring CHARLES KISSINGER — VALERIE ROGERS — TOM BROOKS — D'URVILLE MARTIN AS "THE PIMP"
Executive Producer PHILIP HAZELTON / Produced by GORDON C. LANE & MIKE HENRY / Directed by WILLIAM GIRDER
A GENERAL FILM CORPORATION RELEASE
PG

And another…

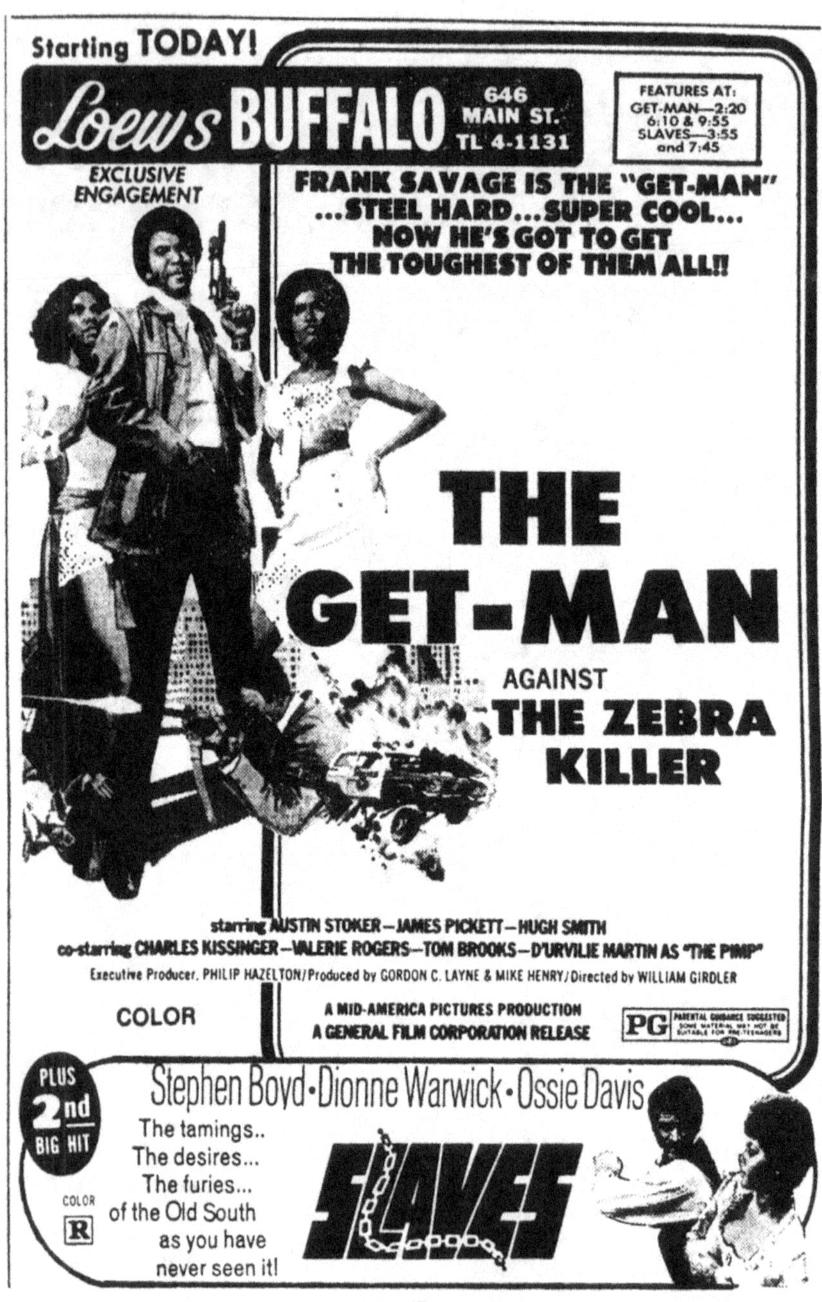

And another, this time with one of the many alternative titles.

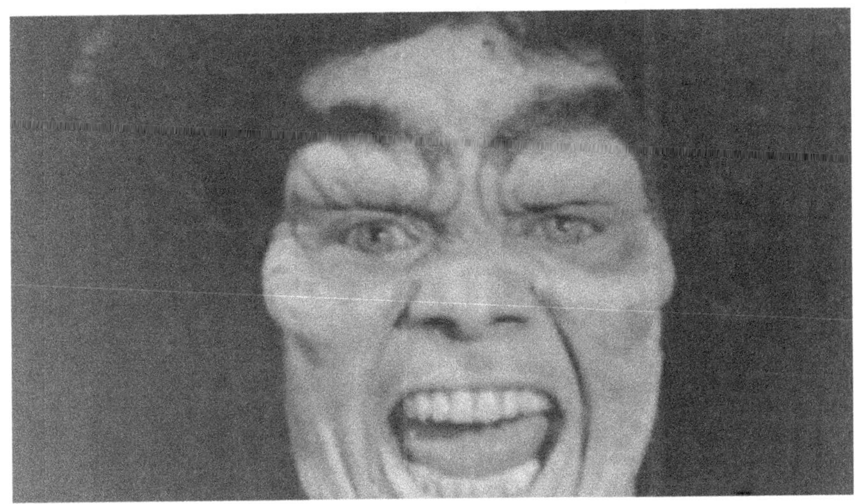

The demon face from Abby.

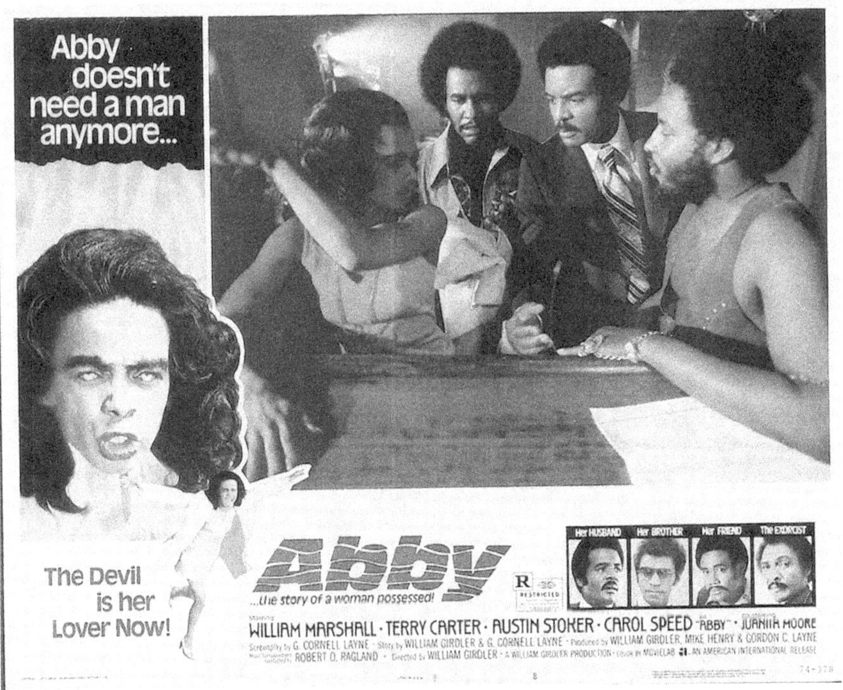

A poster for Abby´s short-lived theatrical run.

Pam Grier is Sheba, Baby.

Leslie Niesen in Project Kill

A very generic action movie ad for Girdler's sixth feature.

A striking example of the ad campaign for Grizzly.

And another...

An unfortunate victim of Grizzly.

The directorial credit on Girdler's biggest hit.

An appropriately ominous title card for Girdler's penultimate feature.

A shocking vision of things to come…

The iconic poster and tagline for Girdler´s last film.

John Cedar and Tony Curtis in The Manitou.

The birth of Misquamacus in The Manitou.

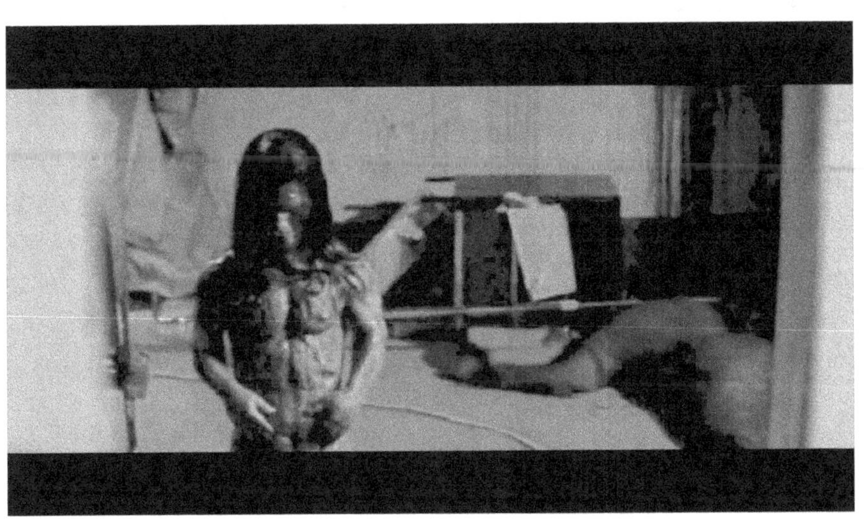

Misquamacus reborn in *The Manitou*.

Chapter 6 - *Sheba, Baby* (1975): Hotter'n "*Coffy*", Meaner'n"*Foxy Brown*"

Synopsis: The film opens with that by-now familiar Girdler setting, Louisville at night and we're right into the exposition. Andy Shayne (Rudy Challenger) runs a loan company and he's being pressured by the gangsters who've put other similar companies out of business. But Andy explains to Brick (Austin Stoker) that he isn't for turning. Given it's a Blaxploitation movie, Andy's belief that things can be worked out without violence seems overtly optimistic. Sure enough, minutes after Rick leaves a group of thugs break into the premises. In a startling indication of just how heavy handed the script is, one of the men states, "Okay, we're just gonna mess the place up a little bit, let them know we mean business". They trash the office and when Andy tries to stop them, he gets a beating. The action shifts to Chicago, where we meet Sheba Shayne (Pam Grier), who's working as a private eye. It turns out that her father's tormenter is small-time hood, Pilot (D'Urville Martin), presumably named after the fish as his gang also includes a Hammerhead, a Whale and a Fin. Sheba teams up with Brick, who is not only her father's partner but also her ex and when the cops (in the shape of Charles Kissinger's Phil) prove themselves to be ineffective in stopping Pilot's hostile takeover, they take matters into their own hands. Or more precisely, hers, Brick is given comparatively little to do while Sheba doles out shootings and beatings. He is keen to rekindle their relationship, though and there's a typically coy Girdler love scene. She gets a lead on Pilot after dunking a suspect's head into powdered chlorine and that night, she confronts him as he counts out his immoral earnings. Brick stops Sheba from killing Pilot, which turns out to be a mistake as he goes on to hire gunmen to stage a raid on Andy's business, after spelling out his philosophical justification for extorting black businesses, offering a cynical twist on black self-reliance; "We've got tough people in the black community, they expect us to take their money". This suggests that African-Americans don't mind getting ripped-off and put out of business as long as it isn't Whitey doing the ripping off. In the raid, Shayne Sr. is shot and Sheba goes full Harry Callahan in an exciting and surprisingly bloody sequence. We see Andy in the hospital and his death is underscored by the lyrics of the song we hear informing us that "a good man is gone". Pilot tries yet again to have Sheba killed but after a chase through a carnival, she forces him (with the threat of decapitation by roller coaster) to give up his boss. It turns out that Pilot is merely doing the bidding of a rich white villain, the aptly-named Shark (the character names are anything but subtle). The openly racist, impeccably groomed Shark has a high-end lifestyle far removed from the mean streets of Louisville and we only see him on the water, either entertaining on his yacht on the Ohio River or fleeing in a speedboat (this may be the reason behind the preponderance of aquatic names). As he tells Sheba, "It's quiet, it gets me away from all that shit in the city". She manages to get an invite to an exclusive party on the yacht, cue a lot of shots of chips being eaten by the seemingly all-white guests. The party is such a non-event, it's hard to know if it's a woeful attempt by the director to depict white decadence – or a satirical observation about just how uptight and middle class this supposed crime kingpin really is. Shark also makes no secret of his disgust for his underling, getting angry when Pilot appears at on the boat ("I told you never to come here… get that trash off my boat"). Pilot ends up tied to the back of a speedboat and drowned by Shark's henchmen. Shark turns out to be, like the straight (white) society he represents, superficially civilized yet corrupt and murderous. His attitude to Sheba manages to be both patronizing and lecherous and part of the pleasure of the film is wondering just how she'll dispatch him. He in turn misses a few opportunities to finish her off, threatening her with various unspoken punishments, tying her up and locking her in the hold (where, stretching credibility somewhat, she finds a large knife someone has left behind). When the cops and Brick arrive, Shark takes off and after a speedboat chase, Sheba kills him with a speargun (his runaway speedboat collides with another boat leading to a big explosion, another instance of the director making the most of AIP's budget).

Pam Grier moved to LA in her late teens and got a job working the switchboard at AIP. The legend has it that she was spotted by the director Jack Hill who cast her in *The Big Doll House* (1971) and *The Big Bird Cage* (1971), a couple of women-in-prison movies shot back-to-back in the Philippines. Hill was an AIP veteran who had co-directed *The Terror* (1963) with Monte Hellman, Francis Coppola and lead actor Jack Nicholson (although canny Roger Corman got the director credit) and worked on a string of patchwork films including co-directing *Blood Bath* (1966) which reused footage from an earlier unreleased spy thriller and the four US/Mexican cheapies which brought Boris Karloff's career to an ignominious end. Away from his compromised work for AIP, he wrote and directed the defiantly weird *Spider Baby* aka *The Maddest Story Ever Told* (1964), which has earned a well-deserved cult following in recent years. Grier, under contract to AIP, went on to play the title roles in Hill's next two films, the blaxploitation thrillers *Coffy* (1973) and *Foxy Brown* (1974). In both films, Grier plays a voluptuous, murderous protagonist seeking revenge on a series of drug pushers and pimps (in stark opposition to other films of the time such as *Superfly* [1972], with its coke-dealing anti-hero). These films made Grier into a Blaxploitation icon who seemed to embody both the requisite sex and violence. Roger Ebert described her as "a young actress of beautiful face and astonishing form" (1973), going on to note how "she also has a kind of physical life to her that is sometimes missing in beautiful actresses. She doesn't seem to be posing or doing the fashion-model bit; she gets into an action role and does it right. And she has great cleavage, too" (Ibid.) It was Sheldon who brought Girdler on board for the latest Grier vehicle:

Then, while I was serving as the temporary head of production at AIP when Larry Gordon left to become president of Columbia Pictures, Sam Arkoff told me he wanted to produce another Pam Grier movie (after the success of Coffee [sic.] and Foxy Brown). I told Sam that I was planning to leave the company, but I had a perfect project for Pam that I intended to produce with William Girdler as director. He asked to see the screenplay (which didn't exist). Bill flew out from Kentucky and we worked all day and night writing the script from scratch so we could have it on Sam's desk in the morning. Sam liked it and we went into production under our Mid-America Pictures banner. Yes, we wrote a screenplay together in one day – David Sheldon.

The project hastily cooked up by Sheldon and Girdler, was *Sheba Baby* and it would end up being the director's fifth feature. Indeed, the tagline frames the film as the third part of a trilogy, underlining the importance not of the director but of the star. While what were arguably the best-known Blaxploitation films were directed by African-Americans (*Sweet Sweetback's Badasssss Song* [1971], *Shaft* [1971], *Blacula*) a number of other films in the cycle were made by white directors, many of whom had form in other areas of the exploitation field. These directors included not only the aforementioned Hill but also Bob Kelljan (*Scream Blacula Scream*), Jack Starrett (*Slaughter* [1972]), Barry Shear [*Across 110*[th] *Street* [1972]), Larry Cohen (*Black Caesar* [1973]), even the British Robert Hartford-Davis (*Black Gunn* [1972]). *Sheba Baby* is certainly the director's most polished film up to that point, although this glossy sheen combined with the lack of sex and some PG-13 violence, makes the film feel at times like a TV movie. A topless scene was left in for the European release but cut for the US and the action is mostly bloodless, especially compared to the R-rated *Coffee* with Sheba dunking one guy's head in a bucket of chlorine and forcing another through a car wash with his window open (!) AIP tended to keep productions costs low but given the kind of budgets Girdler was used to, even this was definitely a step up. He's credited as sole screenwriter but frequent collaborator Sheldon co-wrote the screenplay, a rush job even by indie exploitation standards. It plays on Grier's star persona and her image as a resourceful avenger who always looks stylish, even when stabbing and shooting a succession of creeps, thugs and bad guys. As the song over the opening credits puts it, "She's a dangerous lady who's well put together". Her surname Shayne is significant, evoking *Shane* (1953), George Stevens' iconic film about a hero who rides into town, violently rights a series of wrongs and then leaves again.

There are a few pointed bits of social comment of the kind to be found in many Blaxploitation films, frequently hidden beneath the sensational action and whacky outfits. Our first glimpse of Pilot lounging in bed with a trio of servile, scantily-clad women identifies him as an exploiter of women who'll doubtless get his comeuppance from Sheba, enabling Grier to dole out some of her patented kick-ass feminism (misogynists and racists are asking for it in Grier's work and head villain Shark is both). As Sheba spells out to Andy, "I know you think I'm doing a man's job but I'm not going to sit on the sidelines just because I'm a woman" (again, the screenplay isn't worried about being too on-the-nose).

As in a number of the director's previous films, there are some plot inconsistencies, such as Pilot planting a bomb in Andy's car before he even asks if they can meet (surely it would make more sense to ask first and then plant the bomb if he says no?). But this appears to be a case of credibility sacrificed for the sake of thrills, as Sheba gets into the car only to escape being blown up with seconds to spare (as well as being an excuse to show an explosion). But when a script is written in 24 hours, some plot holes are bound to appear. The ending demonstrates Sheba's continuing independence. Not only does she turn down Brick's offer to stay in Louisville, when he asks her if he can visit, she tells him she'll visit him. The film ends as it begins, with Sheba walking along the mean streets of Chicago, a lascivious shot of her backside er, complicating the film's pretensions to feminism. The film was also a typical family affair. J.

Patrick Kelly is this time round credited as production designer and all three Asman brothers were involved, Bill as director of photography, Bub as an editor and John on sound.

On screen, there's Austin Stoker, Charles Kissinger and – following his cameo in *The Zebra Killer* – D'Urville Martin, seemingly having a ball as the sleazy, hapless Pilot. At one point, he semi-seriously rages at his underlings:

You'd better be right. You'll be pushing up black daisies along with me, you better pray that that broad's daddy don't die or there won't be a safe place for you to shit in this town much less live.

An important figure in Blaxploitation, he appeared in the likes of *The Godfather of Harlem* (1973), *Hell Up in Harlem* (1973) and *The Legend of Nigger Charley* (1973) as well as directing and starring in the popular *Dolemite* (1975). This film, a starring vehicle for the actor-comedian Rudy Ray Moore inspired the 2018 *Dolemite is my Name* which featured Eddie Murphy as Moore and Wesley Snipes as Martin. Outside of the blaxploitation arena, Martin also appeared in *Guess Who's Coming to Dinner* (1967) and played the lift operator in *Rosemary's Baby* (1968). An alcoholic, he died of a heart attack aged 45.

The trailer plays on Grier's star power while also emphasizing the movie's hip credentials:

Sheba Baby, Sheba Baby, Sheba Baby. Pam Grier, that Foxy Brown Coffee gal is Sheba Baby…when you're after the top banana, you peel off the skin…Slammin' Pam, giving the gun brothers the frizzies – and the boss man the tizzies. The heat's on in the street for that big bad mama but she's doin' the cooking and any cat in her way is gonna get fried.

Girdler reportedly clashed with his star and was unhappy with *Sheba Baby* despite the fact that the film was a hit and, as Patricia Breen put it, "the only moneymaking Girdler movie unmarred by legal intrigue" (2000-1). Grier too, didn't seem to be a fan of either the film or its director, "His direction wasn't all that inspired…I had the impression he'd bitten off more than he could chew" (in Dietrich

1975). Her antipathy to Girdler may well have arisen as a result of her successful working relationship with Jack Hill, who relied on her input and regarded her as a collaborator.

Happily, the film still has a small but dedicated cult following in Louisville, being screened at a local "brew-and-view" gathering in 2014. Organizer Todd Brashear of Wild and Woolly Video deserves to be quoted in full as he explains the director's appeal, both to cult films fans and Kentuckians:

"I thought it would be a good movie for people to sit and drink beer to," he says. Brashear believes Louisville natives of a certain age, specifically those who either lived here or grew up here in the '70s, will get a special kick of nostalgia as the movie includes a lot of the local scenery… Such moments of cinematic "I Spy" make the movie fun. "If you grew up in Louisville in the '70s, there's a lot of stuff in the movie to get a person excited," he says. Girdler also cast locals in his movies and used many Louisville-based folks in his crew. Older, sharp-eyed horror fans will recognize Charles Kissinger–who plays Phil in "Sheba, Baby"–as the host of the local horror movie-playing TV show "Fright Night," which used to air on Channel 41, Brashear says. It would be wrong to lump Girdler in with other cult-favorite directors like Ed Wood, who are often loved for how terrible their movies were, Brashear says. Girdler's movies may have been low-budget, but he matured into a skilled craftsman, tackling a variety of topics. "You can't pigeonhole him," he says. "He's not really a 'bad' director." (anon b. 2014).

While Brashear's summing up is a textbook example of damning with faint praise, one gets the feeling that Girdler would be happy that his films are still being watched and enjoyed in his hometown.

Grier got her start with a couple of films shot in the Phillipines, which saw an influx of American independent projects in the 1970s, lured there by the low production costs, experienced crews and exotic locales. It makes sense, therefore that the resourceful Girdler would end up heading out to South-East Asia for his next film.

Chapter 7 - *Project:Kill* (1976): War of the Assassins

Synopsis: The film starts with a group of identically dressed men in a dark room, a projector beam and a leader countdown (an unusually reflexive opening). We see a film-within-a-film with the intertitle informing us we are "somewhere in the United States". There´s some murky footage of an operation which quickly turns into a shooting match, it´s hard to tell what´s going on. There´s a fistfight before a car explodes and a man is engulfed in flames. Then the film stops. We´ve been watching "a reenactment" of an operation being shown to a group of track-suited recruits being given an introductory brief by Temple (Leslie Nielsen) and Lassiter (Gary Lockwood):

This unit, which you´re all so hot to become members of, came about because of events which occurred in the early 60s, it is the only effective means of combatting political assassination by the interception and destruction of the assassin himself.

Members of this elite group have been specially selected and receive "vitamins" and "chemical injections" in order to help them conduct the kind of murky business that always needs doing in the spy thrillers which seemed to proliferate in the mid-70s, doubtless as a response to Watergate and the discovery that governments had no qualms about employing such shady characters as G. Gordon Liddy and E. Howard Hunt. Unlike Liddy and Hunt, Trevor (Leslie Nielsen) has grown disillusioned with his task, indeed, he looks visibly uneasy as he informs the men how they "will become a reflex but highly directed unit of force", able to make a weapon out of "everything from a toenail clipping to a briefcase". He´s also in a bad way physically, withdrawing from drugs and possibly terminally ill, the tingly music we hear on the soundtrack whenever he winces serving as a theme tune for his various ailments. Trevor is especially troubled by the realization that Project Kill is providing not special forces soldiers so much as assassins with a mission to "intercept and destroy" (you'd think that given the name of the project he'd have worked it out earlier, especially as Lassiter asks the men, "What's your project?" and receives the shouted answer, "Kill!")

Like many a disgruntled screen assassin, Trevor may want out but he knows that no-one gets out alive. When Lassiter attempts turn him in, Trevor attacks him and flees, knocking out a couple of security guards as he does so. In Manila he hooks up with a couple of ex-comrades, Carl Wagner (Galen Thompson), the star of that training film, now a burned-out drunk in a wheelchair and the silent Hook (Maurice Downs). Lassiter arrives in Manila and forms an uneasy alliance with Chief Inspector Cruz (Vic Silayan) and an equally uneasy love affair with "US Council liaison Officer" Lynne Walker (Pamela Parsons). Trevor is not only being pursued by the agency and the cops but also by Alok Lee (Vic Diaz), an "international trader" ("Trading in what?" "Anything of value") from Hong Kong. He's superficially charming in a gleaming white suit and sunglasses and is shown as both sadistic and cowardly. He also wants to capture the fugitive and sell his secrets to the highest bidder. Lee's henchmen try a couple of times to kill Lassiter and manage to dispatch Hook and Wagner, torturing the latter for information he won't give up. Meanwhile Trevor meets and is attracted to Lee Su (Nancy Kwan) and – understandably given that he may be dying – he doesn't hang around when it comes to falling in love with her. The day after their relationship is consummated, their drive is interrupted by a couple of Alok Lee's men (who, somewhat improbably, just spot Trevor driving by). This leads to a car chase quickly followed by an attempt on Lassitter's life by the same gang with a hand grenade being set off on his train. Meanwhile Trevor has bigger problems, having to go cold turkey from his unspecified drugs after someone steals his briefcase. The narrative from here on in becomes a series of chases and confrontations which both reinforce (not always successfully) Trevor and Lassiter's fighting skills while allowing Girdler to stage regular action set-pieces. Trevor pays a visit to Herman Kitolis (Mark LeBuse), the man who was supposed to come up with a boat (we can tell he's got a boat because he has a Hemingway-esque sea dog look about him). Lee's men are in the middle of interrogating Kitolis, so Trevor kills them, although this doesn't stop the sailor haggling over money. He also informs Trevor that Wagner is dead. The expository confessions continue, with Trevor telling Lee Su that he's an assassin, a junkie and "not programmed for love". Meanwhile, Alok Lee makes Kitolis lure Trevor into a trap and then cuts the sailor's throat and mutilates his body. It all comes to a head at the docks, where Trevor kills Lee, the cops and Lassiter arrive and the two old friends fight to the death.

We went immediately into *Project: Kill* which I was supposed to direct. We raised our half of the $300,000 budget but our Phillipino co-producer couldn't provide the other half. We were stuck in Manila with a crew and cast but needed to raise the missing half. So I had to give up directing the film and focus on producing and finally got a loan from the Bank of America using our future profits (ha ha) from our former films as collateral – David Sheldon.

Girdler's sixth film may be his most maligned and can certainly be regarded as flawed from the outset. While *Abby* and *Grizzly* were inspired by box-office hits that were also high quality films, *Project:Kill* takes as its source *The Killer Elite* (1975). Being a Sam Peckinpah film, it's not without interest but it's muddled and fragmented, qualities only enhanced by the director's increasing use of cocaine and there's a feeling throughout that Sam can't hide his contempt for the material. As the unhappy star James Caan put it, Peckinpah "had private jokes in there for twenty or thirty of his pals" (in Fine 2005:284). In addition, the film was a minor hit but it fell far short of the grosses for Peckinpah's earlier star vehicle *The Getaway* (1973), never mind the Friedkin and Spielberg pictures.

Girdler's film also fits neatly into a loose collection of mid-70s thrillers which feature some past their peak American stars in far-flung climes including *The Yakuza* (1974), with Robert Mitchum in Japan, *Brannigan* (1974) with John Wayne in London and *Shatter* (1974), one of Hammer's last gasps with Stuart Whitman adrift in

Hong Kong. Indeed, *Project:Kill* features what was Girdler's starriest cast to date. Given Leslie Nielsen's very successful late career shift into comedy with the likes of *The Naked Gun* (1988 – 94), it can be hard to take his straight performances seriously, even in such worthy vehicles as *Forbidden Planet* (1956). He's miscast as stone killer Trevor and is more persuasive showing his more caring side in the romance with Lee Su and the on-off bromance with Lassiter. He's not really up to showing the psychological complexity of a character who's gone from, in Lassiter's words, "a sterile apartment with sterile people around him" to disillusion, drug withdrawal and terminal illness. The moments where he has to show just how brutalized he's become, such as when he wakes up to find himself attacking Lee Su, stopping himself before delivering what we assume will be a killing blow don't convince (Nielsen would go on to play a much more unpleasant character in *Day of the Animals* and there he doesn't disappoint). Still, he turns in a respectable performance, especially when compared to the charisma-free turn from Gary Lockwood as Lassiter. Lockwood's detached, barely-there quality may have been perfect for the chilly *2001:A Space Odyssey* (1968) but here, he just seems bored. In contrast, Galen Thompson is very convincing as a man with a dark past anaesthetizing his demons with cynicism, dark humor and booze. The most affecting moment in the film is when Wagner turns to Hook moments before they're attacked for the last time and asking, "Is today the day?" before pouring their final drinks. Thompson also wrote the screenplay (credited as Donald G. Thompson) based on Sheldon's story and the two men would go on to work on the cult horror film *The Evil* (1978). Born in Hong Kong, Nancy Kwan trained as a ballet dancer before she found stardom in her debut film playing opposite William Holden in *The World of Suzy Wong* (1960). Her filmography throughout the 60s was less than stellar however, consisting of a lot of comedies and routine action fare (the best-known of which was probably the spy spoof *The Wrecking Crew* [1968] which co-starred Dean Martin and Sharon Tate). By the 70s she was making B-movies including *Wonder Women* (1973), also shot in the Philippines and *Supercock* ([1975], not a porno but a comedy about cockfighting). She's given little to do in Girdler's film except look pretty and help humanize the character of Trevor. The Filipino actor Vic Diaz may have started out working for Fritz Lang (making a brief appearance in *American Guerilla in the Philippines* [1950]) but he made his name playing heavies in exploitation films including *Beast of the Yellow Night* (1971), *Black Mama, White Mama* (1972) and *Savage Sisters* (1974). He worked with a number of cult directors including Monte Hellman and Jacks Hill and Starrett and was a reliably charismatic presence, accurately described as "the Filipino Peter Lorre" by Quentin Tarantino (in Po 2020).

The opening shot, a slow pan across the Stars and Stripes accompanied by *faux*-martial music makes clear that although shot in the Philippines, this is a very American story, haunted by the twin specters of Nixon and Vietnam. Trevor is a man who's lost his faith in his mission and his explanation to Lassiter, who doesn't share his doubts, that the Project Kill program involves "more drugs, more mind control" taps into a particular and very topical issue at that time. The CIA's attempts to use various forms of behavior modification, including the use of psychedelic drugs, as weapons led to some extremely unethical and illegal experiments conducted on unsuspecting Americans and managed to make the paranoid fantasy of *The Manchurian Candidate* (1961) seem a lot less fantastical. The files into what was known as MK-Ultra were ordered destroyed by the Director of the CIA in 1973, Richard Helms but public disquiet, post-Watergate, led to various commissions. The extent of these experiments was first made clear in 1975 and so they formed a fertile background for Girdler's film.

The film is much slicker than the director's previous work and contains some flashy fast cutting and striking visual flourishes. One scene of Trevor in a motel room is shot through the blades of a whirling fan, something that not only anticipates similar shots in *Apocalypse Now* (1979) but also the director's death in a helicopter crash which would take place not far away. There's also a lot of very picturesque scenery in marked contrast to Girdler's usual backdrop of night-time Louisville. There are some characteristic touches like the walk in the gardens at the start of Trevor and Lee Su's romance which is reminiscent of similar outings in *Asylum of Satan* and *Three on a Meathook* and yet another of those seemingly interminable m-o-r musical interludes, this time round a ballad titled "Lonely Man", the significance of which is a mite overstated when it plays over the climactic scene of a despondent Lassiter.

The choppily edited fight scenes have been celebrated (if you can call it that) by the kind of people who seek out what they refer to as 'bad cinema' and they certainly pale when compared to similar scenes in *The Killer Elite* (even with his powers waning after years of substance abuse, Sam Peckinpah was a superlative director of action scenes). But in actuality the fights aren't as badly handled as they're rumored to be, even if Nielsen and Lockwood don't really come over as highly trained killing machines. It is notable, though, how the other action scenes, the car chases, gun battles and Lassiter stopping a grenade with a wooden train door are much more effective than the hand-to-hand combat. The ending is a variation on the ending of the Peckinpah, right down to the ocean-front setting with various fights ending with the climactic face-off between the two ex-comrades. Although it's not especially convincing (some half-hearted martial arts moves and falls), the moment when Trevor goads Lassiter into delivering the killing blow in slow-motion accompanied by an amplified scream and the sound of a neck breaking, is a fittingly apocalyptic finale. In a moment typical of the homoeroticism that is a recurring feature in these kind of action films, where the central relationship is between men and the woman stays on the sidelines, Trevor dies looking at Lee Su but holding on to his old friend. Lassiter goes on to throw the case into the sea in the kind of downbeat ending that was popular in both the 70s and Girdler's filmography, a disillusioned protagonist who's reached the end of his string. Indeed here, as in *The Zebra Killer*, the director may have been especially inspired by *Dirty Harry*, which ends with Callahan throwing his shield into water and walking away. Like many exploitation filmmakers, Girdler had to be attuned to what was going on socially and culturally but *Project: Kill* is his most overtly political film, a product of that period of malaise and uncertainty which beset the US after losing a President and an unpopular war. There's a telling exchange between Cruz and Lassiter at the scene of Wagner and Hook's murder:

Cruz: "Carl Wagner. A winner of the Navy Cross for Gallantry in Action. Gallantry, Mr. Lassiter, you know what that word means?"

Lassiter: "Who can afford gallantry these days?"

The moral certainties of World War 2 and the Cold War have disappeared and government man Lassiter, is shown to be no better than Alok Lee's henchmen, just another low-level gangster doing as he's told.

As well as Sheldon, Girdler also recruited his insurance agent and part-time special effects provider (who was also the best man at his first wedding) Joe Schulten and the redoubtable J. Patrick Kelly (listen closely in one of the scenes in the hotel and you'll hear a call come in over the intercom for a "Pat Kelly"). But any commercial hopes there were for this, the most high-profile Girdler film to date were dashed by distribution problems. According to Sheldon, one distributor took too long so the film was picked up by another company, only to have the company director die (some sources suggest suicide but Sheldon has suggested it was a contract killing [See Breen 2000-1]). This led to a certain amount of legal wrangling, which left the film in limbo for years. There isn't even any agreement about the film's release, with some sources claiming it only became available on home video and cable. It's probably the director's most low-profile film but from here on in, his career would move up a couple of leagues. If his first three films, what we might dub "the Kentucky trilogy", were marked by a low-budget, occasionally slipshod but ultimately appealing wildness, his next three features were more polished while also being considerably more anonymous.

For his last three films, what we might refer to as "the Hollywood trilogy", the director would manage to combine his newly acquired technical proficiency with some overheated, highly exploitative content to produce some of his best work.

Chapter 8 - *Grizzly* (1976): The Most Dangerous Jaws on Land!!!

"There's a killer bear out there and I'm sitting around crushing ice cubes in my mouth!"

Synopsis: We open with an establishing shot of spectacular scenery and a speeding helicopter, piloted by Don Stober (Andrew Prine), who gives his passengers (and us) a quick primer on the subject of national parks. The opening credits appear in that bright yellow so evocative of 70s exploitation films (Quentin Tarantino is clearly a fan, what with a number of his films having credits in various shades of that same color) over aerial footage of lakes and forests shot from the very mobile chopper. We're clearly a long way from *Asylum of Satan* this time round. There's some *faux-verité* footage of campers and tourists milling around and at the ranger station, we're introduced to Chief Ranger Michael Kelly (Christopher George). He's concerned about the large amounts of hikers and campers in the park, as that's a lot of protecting and serving for his fellow rangers. We also meet Allison Corwin (Joan McCall), a photographer, daughter of the park hotel proprietor and Kelly's putative love interest. In the park, two young female campers are observed by a subjective camera accompanied by a soundtrack of snuffles, grunts and a rehash of John Williams' repetitive *Jaws* score. When one of the women goes to pee, her companion is killed by the unseen animal which then chases the survivor through the woods. She takes shelter in an abandoned cabin but the momentary calm is shattered when the wall is torn down and she's attacked. Kelly and Allison join the ranger who goes to check on the woman and they discover the bloodied corpse in the damaged shack. The observation from a ranger, "That's all we need, a killer bear on the loose" is a good example of the film's typically blunt dialogue. When Allison wanders off (an unwise choice given the presence of said killer bear), she trips and falls into the half-buried remains of the other victim. The pathologist (Girdler regular Kissinger) suggests that the bear might be a female protecting her cubs but Kelly points out that there was no sign of any cubs at the scene. Park supervisor Kittridge (Joe Dorsey), a stereotypical pen-pushing bureaucrat blames Kelly and the naturalist Arthur "Scotty" Scott (Richard Jaeckel) who apparently knows "every bear in this forest personally" for the attacks because they were supposed to have moved the animals further north away from any tourists. To the accompaniment of a radio news bulletin about the marauding bear, there's a montage of fleeing campers and hikers heading out of the area. The rangers are sent out on a bear hunt and not only do one pair split up, the female ranger also then proceeds to take a shower in a waterfall. One swipe from a giant paw and the water runs red. Kelly and Stober go out in the chopper to see if they can spot the bear and nearly end up shooting Scotty who is tracking deer while disguised in an animal skin. Scotty's enthusiastic about the subject of Grizzlies, relating their prehistoric origins (and while *Arctodus ursus horribilis* sounds terrifying, it didn't really exist.) In a bit of foreshadowing, he mentions how the animals bury their half-eaten prey in shallow graves so they can return to finish them later while his statement that "they just love meat" is followed by an unnerving cut to a camp at night and the sound of children singing. A woman (Sandra Dorsey) leaves her goofy partner and retires to her tent to prepare for sex. Her preparations are rudely interrupted when the bear rips open the tent, lifts her into the air and savages her to a soundtrack of screaming kids. Cue another shouting match between Kelly and Kittridge, the latter unwilling to face the fact that there's a killer bear and instead, putting the blame on tourists leaving food out for the scavenging animals. Against the advice of Kelly and Scotty, Kittridge opens up parts of the park to hunters, leading to a bizarre kind of redneck party with a lot of guns and barking dogs. One lone hunter is stalked by the bear and chased through the forest, only escaping when he falls into a fast-flowing river. Kelly and company have (another!) argument with Kittridge, who dismisses the Ranger as "a maverick."

A group of hunters come across a bear cub and decide to use it as bait but the Grizzly outwits them, circling back and eating the cub. The next day, the animal attacks a spotting tower, bringing it crashing down and killing the ranger in there. Predictably this leads to another of those interminable shouting matches between Kelly and his boss about the need to close the park. Meanwhile in a nearby garden, a young boy is playing with his rabbit. As in the opening of the later *Blue Velvet* (1987), the white picket fence around the garden represents a kind of wholesome normality which is about to be shattered. The bear attacks, ripping off one of the kid's legs and goring the terrified, broom-wielding mother, an alarming sequence that ends with an apocalyptic zoom into the animal's yawning maw. Now even Kittridge understands the park should be closed and our mismatched band of heroes have to set out to kill the bear. But while Kelly and Stober are loading up the chopper, Scotty sets off on horseback to try and capture him alive. For a naturalist, Scotty should surely see that his plan to capture a 15-foot killer Grizzly and lead him out of the forest is foolhardy but this doesn't stop him. Predictably, the bear attacks, decapitating his horse with one blow (a moment which is underplayed, possibly for ratings reasons) and savaging Scotty. The bloodied, unresponsive naturalist is then buried by the bear. When he awakes, he slowly clambers out of his makeshift grave, only to realize that the bear is waiting for him, the dissolve on Scotty's face making his fate clear. Kelly and Stober find his remains, which we don't get a look at and then resume the hunt. There's a cod-philosophical exchange between the two men after they work out that the bear is heading back to the scene of his first kill:

Kelly: It's incredible.

Stober: He's programmed. Like some kind of damned computer.

Kelly: How, why, man?

Stober: I don't know. Why do salmon swim back upstream to where it all began?

They finally spot the animal, leading to a chopper vs. bear chase through the forest. When they land, the bear attacks the helicopter and Don shoots it repeatedly with little effect. Instead of doing the sensible thing and running away, he uses the rifle as a club and is, somewhat predictably, killed. In a faintly ridiculous but undoubtedly crowd-pleasing finale, Kelly shoots the bear with a bazooka, leaving just a patch of burning grass where it stood. The fact that Kelly walks away from the remains of the bear without extinguishing the flames (he is a forest ranger after all) underlines the film's view of him as the lone Western hero striding of into the sunset, although not before appearing to at least check if Stober is dead.

The theory of evolution puts man in the position of an ageing South American dictator. The world is full of pushy species, any one of which might be preening itself as our successor (Newman 1988:65).

The Animals Attack sub-genre was around in various forms before the 1970s. There were the rampaging army ants in *The Naked Jungle* (1954) and a handful of horror films featuring killer creatures including *Black Zoo* (1963) and *The Deadly Bees* (1966). More influential was the Big Bug 50s sci fi cycle which saw the giant ants of *Them* (1954), the titular *Tarantula* (1955) and even *The Killer Shrews* (1959). When the animals didn't get bigger, the human got smaller, with *The Incredible Shrinking Man* (1957) menaced by a cat and a truly terrifying spider. The key Animal Attack text is undoubtedly Hitchcock's *The Birds* (1962), a technically innovative apocalyptic science fiction film about unexplained avian attacks in a small Californian town. The disturbing open ending, which offers little closure and ensures the world stays out of balance, would prove extremely influential a decade later. The 1970s saw a boom in such films arising from two major factors. Firstly, exploitation filmmakers were keen to cash in on the anxieties around pollution and environmental damage, as in *Frogs*, a key entry in the Eco-Horror cycle where a number of species descend on the Florida mansion of rich businessman Ray Milland to punish him for his polluting ways. George McCowan's film was also the first feature David Sheldon worked on and there's a clear line from *Frogs* to the Girdler Animal Attack films.

Bill and I split up amicably because, again, I wanted to direct but had to do the producing. Later on, when Bill saw a script of Grizzly, which I wrote with Harvey Flaxman, on my desk (we both had offices at the Goldwyn Studios in Hollywood) he asked me what it was about. He loved it and said he could get Ed Montoro at Film Ventures to finance and distribute it. But only if he would direct it. I almost had a deal for it at Warner Brothers, but (bird in hand) I went with Montoro. Within 3 weeks of casting we were into pre-production in the mountains of Georgia – David Sheldon.

The fears of nature striking back weren't just confined to the screen, what with Africanized Killer Bees joining nuclear accidents, muggers, terrorists and serial killers as one of the 1970s existential threats. Even more important was the unprecedented box office success of *Jaws* which led to a dramatic proliferation in Nature's Revenge horror films, from the glossy *Orca, Killer Whale* (1977) with Richard Harris and Charlotte Rampling to the numerous bargain basement sharksploitation films, often made by tried and tested rip-off merchants. These included *Mako:Jaws of Death* (1976) from William Grefe, *Tintorera* (1977) from Rene Cardona Jr and a cluster of low-budget Italian offerings. Lucio Fulci's *Zombie Flesh Eaters* (1979) managed to combine George Romero and Spielberg in the remarkable scene where one of the undead has an underwater fight with a shark. It isn't hard to see why *Jaws* proved so appealing to exploitation filmmakers, being both an unprecedented box office smash and a monster movie. Indeed, Spielberg's direction and the impressive cast help elevate a film which owes more to *Creature from the Black Lagoon* (1954) than it does *Moby Dick* (1851). The fast-paced narrative, an exciting combination of Hitchcock-style scares, action-adventure riffs and a monster, would prove influential and the film wasn't above providing some effectively lurid shock moments such as the bloody death of 12-year-old Alex Kintner and the sudden appearance of a severed head.

The ecological concerns of the 1970s would play a large part in Girdler's next film, another tale of nature striking back but in the case of *Grizzly*, it's clear that Spielberg's shark is the primary influence. Exhibit a is the tagline describing Girdler's film as "the most dangerous jaws in the land" although the alternate tagline, "18 feet of gut-crunching fury" was much more impressive. At one point, Kissinger's pathologist suggests that the first two victims might have been killed by a mother bear after they disturbed her cubs but the Grizzly has nowhere near as prosaic a motive for his mayhem. Indeed, like Bruce the shark he's less a predatory animal than he is a killing machine, the kind of implacable threat that turns up in many a 70s movie, be it the natural catastrophe of *Earthquake* (1974), Charles Bronson in *Death Wish* (1974) or Leatherface. It's also something that crops up in a many a Spielberg film, from the truck in *Duel* (1971) to the T-Rex in *Jurasssic Park* (1993), perhaps even Amon Göth who murders random Jews during breakfast in *Schindler's List* (1993). Girdler's Grizzly is the kind of remorseless, endlessly resourceful enemy (described at one point by Kelly as seeming "to know what we're thinking") which has roots that go back to Robert Mitchum's phony Preacher in *Night of the Hunter* (1955) and Yul Brynner's robot gunman in *Westworld* (1973) and would become a staple in big-budget science fiction films such as *Alien* (1979), *The Terminator* (1984) and *Predator* (1987). The moment towards the end of *Grizzly*, where Stober attacks the bear armed only with an empty rifle seems to be another lift from Spielberg. The pilot is killed with blood running out of his mouth largely because that's how Quint is killed off. But the official story of *Grizzly*'s origins curiously omits any mention of *Jaws*. Instead, Harvey Flaxman and Sheldon have repeatedly insisted that the story was inspired by the former's encounter with a scary bear on a cross-country trip. This doesn't really explain why, if this really was the case, the script follows the *Jaws* template virtually beat for beat.

Well, for Grizzly we had no script. My agent called me up and said, "They're paying this amount of money. You're getting on a plane tomorrow. And you're going to Clayton, Georgia in the Smokey Mountains." And I said, "What do you mean? What's the script?" He said, "The script is Jaws. They're writing it. Go. Get going. They're going to start paying you tomorrow. And you're the captain from Jaws." (Prine in Kitley 2016).

While Spielberg had Scheider, Dreyfuss and Shaw, Girdler has George, Prine and Jaeckel, who had appeared on-screen together in an earlier film, the John Wayne vehicle *Chisum* (1970). George is Kelly (a role Clint Walker turned down), the Brody character, Jaeckel's Scott is a combination of Hooper and Quint, a naturalist, bear expert *and* macho eccentric while Prine's Stober, good ol' boy, Vietnam vet and daredevil helicopter pilot adds a sardonic smartass quality to proceedings. Fittingly for a Korean War veteran, George found fame as the star of the WW2 drama *The Rat Patrol* (1966 – 8) and he appeared in a number of exploitation films in the 70s including the Corman picture, *I Escaped from Devil's Island* (1973), a Girdler-esque rip-off of a major studio film, in this case, *Papillon* (1973). He'd return for Girdler's next film before dying in 1983 aged 52. One big difference between the two films is the relationship between the beleaguered protagonist and the wider society. Spielberg's film owes much to Ibsen's *Enemy of the People* (1882) with its themes of unwilling martyrdom and social alienation. Brody, like Ibsen's Dr. Stockmann, is a reputable member of society whose zealous insistence on the truth leads him to be shunned. But Chief Ranger Kelly is much more of a renegade, a very American archetype of a man alone against pen-pushing corporate bureaucracy. As Kittridge puts it, "You're a maverick. We don't have room for mavericks". Kelly is, like countless Western heroes and rogue cops before him, an outsider raging against the system. He's not the first such character in the director's filmography, what with the rule-breaking (and remarkably ineffective) cop Frank Savage in *The Zebra Killer* and the disillusioned operative Trevor in *Project:Kill*, as the theme song to the latter film has it, the "lonely man". Like Westerns and cop thrillers, this is a very male story, as evidenced in the way Kelly turns his back on any potential romance with Allison, dismissing the idea as "little boy and girl games". What a man's gotta do…

Jaeckel's filmography was much more interesting, a lot of war films and Westerns, a handful of tough action movies for Robert Aldrich (he helped to train *The Dirty Dozen* [1968]) and Peckinpah's *Pat Garrett and Billy the Kid* (1973). He also turned up in *Mako: Jaws of Death*. As the eccentric naturalist, Jaeckal largely underplays it, making good use of those expressive eyes.

Prine, meanwhile, has some serious cult credentials, making a string of interesting low-budget genre films including *Simon, King of Witches* (1971), *Nightmare Circus* aka *Barn of the Naked Dead* ([1974], directed by Alan Rudolph!), *The Town That Dreaded Sundown* (1978) and another Sheldon project, *The Evil*. Prine possesses a Peter Fonda-ish kind of cool, remaining largely nonplussed by the antics of the killer bear. When he's told the animal "likes women and moves around a lot", he quips "like me". In his best scene, he delivers a campfire monologue – an ursine variation on Quint's USS Indianapolis speech, the story of a villageful of Native Americans eaten by bears – which the actor wrote himself:

Stober: So then you had a situation. A whole herd of man-eating Grizzlies just

parading around, tearing up Indians.

Scott: That's pretty hard to believe.

Stober: Unless you happen to be one of them Indians.

This suggestion that Stober may be at least part-Native American is, like so many other interesting plot threads in the Girdler *oeuvre* left dangling, partly as a result of the fast turnaround times and also, one always gets the impression, that he's not *so* interested in anything that slowed down the thrust of the narrative.

That late night self-penned monologue wasn't the only thing Prine had in common with Robert Shaw, both men spending a lot of the time on their respective shoots drunk. As Prine told an audience at the New Beverly during a post-screening Q&A, "I did a lot of drinking on that set…So I went over to the bear's keeper and I said,

"What's he trained to do?" and he tells me, "Mister, this bear ain't trained". This is clearly a tall tale but Prine is quite the raconteur and as the saying goes, when the legend becomes fact print the legend. His character also gets an anti-war speech as they load up the chopper for the final confrontation with the bear which can't help but call to mind the similar speech in *Three on a Meathook*:

Y'know in Nam I zapped about a hundred, maybe two hundred gooks. People. We called 'em gooks so it wouldn't get personal. But it did get personal anyway so I stopped counting and tried to stop caring.

Off-screen, Prine was involved in a real-life mystery which is much discussed by conspiracy theorists and scandal fetishists, one of whom, crime writer and self-proclaimed "Demon Dog" of American crime fiction, James Ellroy wrote an essay about it (see Ellroy 1999). Prine had a relationship with a bit-part actor called Karyn Kupcinet who was found naked and dead in her West Hollywood apartment on November 28th 1963, six days after the Kennedy assassination. Although it wasn't clear if Kupcinet had been murdered – indeed, Ellroy considers her death a weird accident – the police considered Prine a suspect, along with a number of other men. Since her death, some conspiracy theorists have suggested she was the mysterious female caller who tried to warn authorities of a plot to kill the President and was murdered in turn but there's very little substance to these rumors. Kupcinet's death remains a mystery.

While Clint Walker would probably have worked better than George in the film, Prine's role was originally offered to Ben Johnson, something which would've called for some hasty rewriting (Johnson was 17 years older than Prine and too old to convince as a skirt-chasing hotshot Nam veteran). In *Grizzly*, Prine stands out as an oasis of laconic cool amongst all the histrionics, George in particular being prone to delivering his lines in a shout and coming over as merely belligerent rather than impassioned. The same is true of Joe Dorsey, normally a reliable performer who made a string of notable films (*Norma Rae* [1979], *Wise Blood* [1979]). His Kittridge is clearly modeled on Murray Hamilton's Mayor Vaughn in the Spielberg film but whereas the latter is allowed some humanity, Dorsey is just required to yell and impotently rage at his insubordinate Chief Ranger. It would've been interesting to see what Kissinger, here wasted in what is pretty much a glorified cameo, would've done with the role. Joan McCall, meanwhile, is given little to do, in large part because as an action picture it's very testosterone-heavy (even the bear is male). As well as acting, McCall is a prolific screenwriter of daytime soaps and along with husband Sheldon, she would write the screenplay for *Grizzly*'s troubled, long-gestated sequel. The woman killed in the shack was played by Kathy Rickman, who'd had a small role in another rural survival story (possibly *the* rural survival story), *Deliverance*. She was the daughter of the real-life "Mountain Man" Frank Rickman, a larger-than-life character who ended up, somewhat incongruously, working for the Georgia Film Commission. One of the oft-repeated stories about *Grizzly* involves another *Jaws* connection, that the unfortunate ranger killed in the waterfall was played by Susan Backlinie, who played the first victim of the killer shark but although it's still out there, it isn't true. The ranger was Victoria Johnson, a "Penthouse Pet" who also appeared as Angie Dickinson's body double in *Dressed to Kill* (1980). She also did the waterfall scene nude to provide some alternate footage for overseas cuts of the film.

The main location was a national park in Clayton, Georgia, a town which was also the location for a very different animal adventure, Disney's *Old Yeller* (1957). The park, unnamed in the film, offers a spectacular backdrop to what is easily Girdler's most handsome film yet. While William Asman's cinematography is a bit murky in the night-time scenes, there is some stunning footage of the landscape, the dense forest and wide-open spaces.

Seen now, the film not only lifts heavily from Spielberg but also, like a number of other Girdlers, anticipates the slasher movie. There are regular bloody killings, many of them accompanied by a prowling subjective camera and the isolated rural setting is the same kind of picturesque slayground that would feature in *Friday the 13*[th] and its many sequels and imitators. Before the first attack, there's the kind of bait and switch which would become a staple of the sub-genre, with a rustling in the bushes turning out to be a ranger on horseback, a moment of relief, which is quickly followed by bloody mayhem. The bear is often shown to be killing for the sheer joy of it rather than for food, as in the scene where he savages the woman at the campsite. He doesn't consume any of her, simply grabbing and goring her before dropping her body on the ground. Similarly, the moment the bear silently waits for Scotty to dig himself out of the ground before striking is more Jason Voorhees than *ursus horribilis.* The fixation on the gory aftermath of the bear attacks, the tumbling body in the shack, the half-eaten body which Alison falls on top of, have a distinctly horrific tone (while slasher movies foreground the act of killing, there's also a grim pleasure to be had in the discovery of the numerous corpses). As Kelly puts it, "it's a butcher's shop out there". The amount of carnage in the film proved a problem when it came to securing that all-important family rating. The film was submitted three times to the MPAA and was certificated PG after some of the bloody excesses were trimmed. In the UK, the British Board of Film Classification also insisted on cuts (to the scene where the kid is attacked as well as some bloodied faces and severed body parts) before granting the film the non-restrictive A rating. Appropriately enough, the same rating was also handed out to *Jaws.* In both territories, the film can now be seen as intended albeit with more restrictive ratings (R in the US, 15 in the UK).

Contrary to Prine's claims, bear trainer Terry Rowland in a filmed interview describes Teddy the bear as having been "a movie star all his life, this is just another job for him". He wasn't actually a Grizzly but rather a Kodiak and although he's described in the film as fifteen feet tall, he was in actuality a still pretty intimidating eleven feet. In classic exploitation tradition, the poster tagline ups the ante and declares him to be "18 Feet of Gut-Crunching Fury".

Certainly, the use of a real animal means Girdler manages to one-up the sometimes patently fake shark of the earlier film. But those same special effects limitations led to Spielberg's extremely effective cinematic tricks including scenes shot at the waterline and that subjective camera lurking beneath the surface. In contrast the bear point-of-view shots are far more conventional with the director using a technique he'd previously tried out in *Three on a Meathook*. Having a potentially dangerous wild animal on the set, even one who was a veteran "movie star", called for some fairly elaborate arrangements including the construction of a fake electric fence from green string and a ticking alarm clock (primitive but convincing enough to fool Teddy). The shots of the bear on the attack complete with yawning maw were achieved by tossing marshmallows to him. There are a couple of scenes where it's clearly not Teddy, such as the large paw used to kill the ranger in the waterfall and the giant fake bear which savages the kid and kills Stober. Photos taken of this fake indicate just how successful Girdler was in disguising it, seeing as it looks very like a large teddy bear (as opposed to Teddy the bear).

Given *Grizzly*'s heavy er, borrowings from *Jaws*, it isn't a surprise to find Edward Montoro involved in the production. Montoro was, maybe still is, an enigmatic figure, a pilot who entered the film business in his early 40s after a plane crash. His company, Film Ventures International initially specialized in softcore sexploitation and Italian imports, the likes of *X-Rated Girl* (1971) and *Boot Hill* (1969), a Terence Hill/Bud Spencer Western. Montoro's work as director was very much in that mold, with his Uschi Digard romp *Getting Into Heaven* (1970), summarized on IMDb as, "Miss Heaven wishes very much to get into films, but first she must meet Sin through Salacity, that is, have all sorts of sex on a producer's couch". FVI had a big hit with the aforementioned Italian *Exorcist* clone, *Beyond the Door* and unlike Girdler, they managed to fend off a lawsuit from Warners. Much the same as Girdler and co, FVI was originally based far from Hollywood, in

Atlanta, Georgia and unlike Roger Corman, Montoro had no pretensions to artistry, happy to be making films for what he referred to as "the mug house crowd" (Vorel 2017), young filmgoers looking for cheap thrills. As Rick Alpert, an entertainment lawyer and FVI collaborator put it:

Corman would get *Kagemusha* and these really high-class films to distribute. Ed was not like that. People in L.A. would call him the Beverly Hillbilly who came from the sticks, because he came out here and lived the same way. He used to say, 'The mug house crowd will always go out to see these horror films. They gotta go see them; the market for them will never disappear.' And that market is still there today, so he was right. (in Vorel 2017).

Grizzly was one of the few films FVI produced in-house and it was an enormous success, in large part because it was one of the first of the host of *Jaws* rip-offs. It cost an estimated $750,000 and ended up making a staggering $39 million profit. But the relationship between the director and producer soured over a court case, although surprisingly, this time round it wasn't an *Abby*-style plagiarism suit. On the spurious grounds that the film had gone over-budget, Montoro decided he was going to keep all of the profits for himself. Flaxman, Sheldon and Girdler sued to get their share, although by the time the suit was settled in their favor the director was dead.

Despite this major blip in their relationship, Girdler and Montoro would team up again for *Day of the Animals*, which was based on the producer's story.

I had a particularly strange experience on the film [*Day of the Animals*]. There was a dinner scheduled at a lodge or restaurant a good distance from our Motel. I was for some reason relegated to riding back to the motel with a drunken Edward L. Montororo (sic.) – babbling unintelligibly – careening down winding, unlit mountain roads and 2-lane curves – like an inebriated Mr. Toad with a Moe Axelrod mustache – I survived – but he remains the subject of speculation after his embezzlement of Film Ventures International and disappearance – never to be heard from again. Dead or Alive who knows? – Andrew Stevens.

After his second collaboration with Girdler, Montoro had a hand in a string of cult horror pictures including *The Visitor* ([1979] with an oddball cast which included Glenn Ford, Sam Peckinpah, Shelley Winters and John Huston!), *Don't Go in the House* and *Pieces* (1982). But his habit of ripping off blockbusters got him into trouble (again) when FVI released the Italian sharksploitation cheapie *Great White* aka *The Last Shark/L'ultimo squalo* (1981), accompanied by a huge publicity drive (including putting a pool of live sharks in Caesar's Palace). Universal tried to block the release of the film, alleging copyright infringement (and who could blame them?) but the suit failed and although it was critically mauled, *Great White* was a commercial success, making $18 million in its first month. But after a second judgement went against FVI, the film was pulled from cinemas and Universal took possession of the prints. This backstory is considerably more interesting that the film itself, which is weak even by the already-pretty-low sharksploitation standards. In a clear indication of the exploitation world's tendency to self-cannibalize, bits of the film would end up alongside extracts from *Jaws* in yet another Italian rip-off *Cruel Jaws* (1995), also known as *Jaws 5:Cruel Jaws*. In 1984, following health problems and with a divorce pending, Montoro disappeared with more than a million dollars in cash, more than likely heading for Mexico and he hasn't been seen since. If he's still alive, he'll be 88 years old.

One sign of *Grizzly*'s higher profile – certainly compared to grindhouse fodder like *Meathook* and *The Zebra Killer* – is the existence of a *Making Of* promo film financed by FVI. Clearly intended as an advertisement, seen now it's a fascinating document of Girdler at work. Over shots of the wilderness, we're told how:

Most motion picture crews enjoy the comfort and conveniences of shooting on soundstages and backlots. But director William Girdler recently took his crew on location deep into the hills of

Georgia, sometimes actually making their own roads to film deeper…into the wilderness.

Girdler, wearing a moustache, heavy parka and sunglasses throughout, comes over as the driven auteur, both complaining about and celebrating the hardships involved in the film-making process. Most of the almost eight-minute running time is made up of clips but there's an interview with Terry Rowland, one of Teddy's trainers and some snapshots of the copter chase and the construction and destruction of the spotting tower.

When *Grizzly* was released, Girdler's hometown paper was begrudging rather than simply dismissive:

"Grizzly" isn't going to make anyone's list of "10 Best Films of 1976" but I doubt if Girdler could care less, I imagine he'll be satisfied if a lot of shark-fans will pay $3.50 to become bear-fans. And "Grizzly" is just effective enough that I see no reason why that shouldn't happen (Hammen 1976).

Alongside the PG classification at the foot of the review was a note, presumably for parents, informing them that "There's a lot of blood and some dismembered limbs but if it didn't offend you when the shark did it, you won't hold it against a bear" (Ibid.) On this latter point, Vincent Canby in The New York Times disagreed:

"Grizzly" is not only clumsily plotted, photographed and edited, it is also downright rude when it insists on showing us the bear lopping off an arm or decapitating a horse. Because it's not good enough to earn the right to scare us, I would hope intelligent adults would avoid it and that parents would give it a personal X. Officially it's been rated PG (Canby 1976).

In a classic case of exploitation cinema eating itself, Girdler's *Jaws* rip-off would itself be ripped-off by *Claws* (1977), the story of a Grizzly rampaging around Juneau, Alaska. This was another gig for bear trainer Monty Cox and a pretty good illustration of the laws of diminishing returns.

The Strange Case of *Grizzly 2: Revenge.*

Also known as *Grizzly 2: The Concert*, this belated sequel to Girdler's film has quite the backstory. Producer Suzanne C. Nagy acquired the sequel rights and the film was shot in Hungary in 1983. At least, some of it was, 45 days of principal photography directed by the Hungarian André Szöts, better-known as a producer with a diverse back catalogue (from the respectable *Cyrano De Bergerac* [1990] starring Gerard Depardieu to the not-so-respectable *Laura* [1979], a slice of soft-focus erotica by David Hamilton). Co-producer Joseph Ford Proctor disappeared early in the shoot and was later jailed for five years for tax fraud. The footage lay around for more than two decades until a poor quality workprint was released online, creating a small-scale buzz amongst the more rabid cult film fans. In 2018, Nagy had the copy removed from various websites and extra footage was shot, the complete version being released in 2020. The screenplay is credited to husband-and-wife team David Sheldon and Joan McCall and the story is a thin rehash of the first film with a Mama Grizzly rampaging through a national park about to play host to a music festival. It boasts an unusually eclectic cast which includes Louise Fletcher, Timothy Spall, Ian McNeice and Jack Starrett, all of whom are too good to be appearing in this sort of thing (Starrett, who in addition to acting was a director of exciting exploitation movies including *Race with the Devil* and *The Strange Vengeance of Rosalie* [1972] would've made a much better job of *Grizzly 2* than Szöts did). In a move which can be regarded as foolhardy or just plain cynical, the top-billed performers are George Clooney, Charlie Sheen and Laura Dern. The trio appear briefly at the start in footage shot in 1983 (Sheen looks about 12) and are swiftly dispatched by the patently fake bear. There's an amateurish, slapdash quality to the whole thing, mismatched scenes, choppy editing and an appearance by the 80s pop band Toto Coelo. Director Szöts and stars Starrett, Deborah Raffin and Dick Anthony Williams all died before the film's eventual release. As with *Dr. Gore* aka *Body Shop*, the miserable *Grizzly 2* is an excellent riposte to anyone who thinks Girdler lacked talent. Compared to Szöts, he's Kubrick.

While Girdler's *Grizzly* was an enormous hit, its success was down to a number of factors, only one of which was the director. Far more important was the timing, following so close on the heels on Spielberg and coming just before the glut of similar eco horrors.

As David Flint wrote, it's:

a film that succeeded by doing exactly what it was supposed to, but there is no real directorial stamp on the project. It was, ultimately, another step up the ladder for its young director, but his career was going to carry on steadily climbing rather than leaping forward, and his next film would be a continuation of the themes explored in **Grizzly**, with some of the same stars but a much more original plot (Flint 2021).

That next film was...

Chapter 9 - *Day of the Animals* (1977): For Centuries, They were Hunted for Bounty, Fun and Food...Now it's Their Turn!

AKA *Something is Out There*.

"This is just terrific. Animals biting people and there's no food"

Synopsis: The film opens with a text informing us about the relatively recent (1974) discovery that the ozone layer was being damaged by the widespread use of aerosols. Exploitation film-making is transformed into gloomy prophecy when we're informed, 'This motion picture dramatizes what COULD happen in the near future IF we continue to do nothing to stop this damage to Nature's protective shield for life on this planet'. In Northern California, a disparate group of hikers set off on a mountain trek led by Steve Buckner (Christopher George) and Native American guide Daniel Santee (Michael Ansara). In an attempt to create the authentic hiking experience, they take no food – planning on collecting some at various points in the journey – and no weapons. Steve is warned not to go by a local (the kind of warning familiar from the local peasants in Dracula films and one that would be echoed by the predictions of doom from Crazy Ralph in *Friday the 13*[th]). In keeping with the disaster movies popular in the 1970s, the hikers can conveniently be divided into types, right down to being played by a host of vaguely familiar faces including a handful of Girdler regulars. The attractive reporter Terry Marsh (Lynda Day George), the bespectacled Professor MacGregor (Richard Jaeckel), the careerist lawyer Frank Young (Jon Cedar) and his unhappy wife Mandy (Susan Backlinie), teenage lovers, Bob Denning (Andrew Stevens) and Beth Hughes (Kathleen Hughes), Beverly Hills socialite Shirley Goodwyn (Ruth Roman) and young son Johnny (Bobby Porter), retired football player, Roy Moore (Paul Mantee) who's hiding a terminal cancer diagnosis and the casually racist would-be alpha male advertising executive, Paul Jenson (Leslie Nielsen). This last character, a white-collar urbanite trying to prove himself manly in the great outdoors feels like a nod to the aforementioned *Deliverance*. The radio station reports unusual animal behavior on the mountain and back in town, locals including the Sheriff gather in Murphy's Hotel and discuss the subject in a scene clearly derived from a similar set piece in *The Birds*, right down to the character in both films who regards the animal attacks as divine judgement (in the Hitchcock it's a zealous Christian, in the Girdler it's a character called Sam who declares, "God sent a plague down on us because we're just a bunch of no good fellows").

The hikers happen upon a deserted camp site and – perhaps unwisely – decide to sleep nearby. In the night, Mandy is attacked in her sleeping bag by wolves and any student of Girdler – or indeed, animal attack films – won't be surprised to find this first victim is played by Backlinie who a couple of years earlier had appeared as Chrissie Watkins, the iconic first victim of Bruce the mechanical Great White. It's decided that the wounded woman and her husband should head back down the mountain to the nearest ranger station at daybreak. But on their way down the mountain, Mandy and Frank find themselves stalked by birds of prey that attack her, sending her plunging off a cliff to her death. An argument between Shirley and her young son leads to the radio being broken, isolating the party even more. That, and the food they were supposed to be collecting *en route* has been eaten by foraging animals. The fleeing Frank meets a young girl "aged about 6 or 7" we're later told, who is mute, seemingly due to trauma and the two of them team up. Meanwhile back in town, the army have been deployed to oversee the evacuation of the townsfolk and the Sheriff is threatened by a fierce stray dog and then attacked in his kitchen by some hungry rats. The town is duly evacuated and there are plans made to rescue the Buckner party. That night on the mountain, the campers are attacked by mountain lions. This leads to the kind of plot development familiar from *Night of the Living Dead* and any number of disaster movies as the group divide up into two factions amid a power struggle between Buckner and the increasingly unhinged Jenson (who, like the animals, appears to be affected by the ozone depletion although it's never made clear if this is the case and if so, why it's just him). The angry ad-man decides to lead his group further up the mountain looking for another of those elusive ranger stations. Meanwhile, Frank and the girl discover a campsite but any relief they feel is predictably short-lived when they discover it's abandoned with the few belongings left behind strewn around. That night there's a thunderstorm and while Buckner's group shelter in an old mineshaft, higher up the mountain, Jenson has become tyrannical, strutting around giving orders while shirtless and wielding a big stick. He attacks Beth, intent on raping her and when Bob tries to intervene he ends up impaled by the ad-man's stick. Shirley and her son try to attack Jenson but an angry bear appears at the base and when the insane ad-man tries to fight the animal he is (unsurprisingly) killed. His line earlier about campers being "bear-bait" turned out to have been a prescient one.

In the morning, Frank and the Girl enter the eerily-deserted village and find an Army truck manned by a dead man with a snake-bitten face. Frank hides the Girl in a vehicle but his attempt to reassure her ("We're going to be alright") pretty much guarantees that they won't be. When he tries to take a car, he finds it's full of snakes and he's bitten and then attacked by a fierce dog, all of this happening in front of the Girl. The survivors of the Jenson party continue on their way. They find an abandoned helicopter with the dead pilot being devoured by dogs. They're then forced to take refuge in the copter when pumas attack. The Buckner party are hiding in a dilapidated cabin when a gang of dogs attack, a German Shepherd somewhat improbably leaping through a window to get at them. The Professor and Moore are killed but the other three escape. They manage to flee downriver on a makeshift raft but the dogs manage to get on board as the river gets increasingly wild.

The party in the copter awake to find everything is calm and all of the animals have died, their bodies scattered around. They are rescued by another helicopter. In town, a group of soldiers in protective suits arrive to find the place littered with dead animals and their human victims. A radio broadcast informs us that the same atmospheric conditions that caused the animals to become crazed has ended up killing them. The Girl is rescued and the survivors of the Buckner party wake up on their drifting raft to discover order has been restored. The last line of dialogue is Terry's "It's over" but this is undercut by the final image, a screeching hawk captured in a freeze-frame which suggests that humanity's respite may not last long…

It's clear from the outset that *Day of the Animals* is going to be Girdler's most accomplished film to date. The cinematography is so much better than the earlier films, there's a powerful score from Lalo Schifrin and a pleasingly unnerving tone, right from that opening dissolve from the sun to an eagle eye, the premise neatly summed up in seconds. The credits are played out over sun flares and a veritable menagerie, birds, a bear, a spider, a wolf, a puma.

Christopher George, Jaeckel and Nielsen had all worked with the director before and Cedar and Ansara would both on to work on *The Manitou*. Andrew Prine was offered a role but turned it down, telling the director "I'm not going to be killed by a rabid squirrel" (Prine in Kitley 2016). The best-known member of the cast is Ruth Roman, who had starred in a number of prestige films including Hitchcock's *Strangers on a Train* (1945). By the 1970s, like many a veteran performer, she was toiling in the exploitation arena, although a couple of these films, *The Baby* (1973) and *The Killing Kind* (1974) were better than the vast majority of her earlier studio work.

The characters are, at first glance, broadly-drawn and easily identifiable. Buckner, the laconic tough guy, Terry the glamorous blonde news presenter, the Professor bespectacled and thoughtful and Shirley the rich divorcee missing her creature comforts. But as the film goes on, the characters are allowed to display more depth.

Terry, for example, turns out to be a very 70s independent woman, telling Steve that her interest in reporting came about because of a brief affair she had with one of her college professors who taught the subject. It's also significant that the member of the party who's transformed by the ozone depletion isn't the football player or the teenager but the white-collar professional. This taps into a then-popular suspicion towards The Man and the straight society he represents. The fact that Jenson is supposed to have worked on the anti-pollution ad from the Keep America Beautiful organization showing "the Indian with the tear in his eye" is not only ironic, given his frequent racist remarks to Santee but also underlines the ecological concerns of the film.

Like Girdler's previous outing, the film anticipates the "who will survive and what will be left of them" narratives of the slasher cycle which would come to dominate the genre in a few years as we watch one character after another get killed off by different species. Indeed, the alternative title, *Something is Out There* sounds like it belongs to a stalk and slash film. The bird attack on Mandy is very well-mounted although the moment when she falls to her death is spoiled by poor optical work. By contrast, Jenson vs the bear is a bit of a let-down. Given that the viewer will have been waiting for the arrogant ad-man to get his comeuppance, it seems odd to make his death much less harrowing than the death of poor Mandy. It's suggested that not only are the animals hunting humans but they're also teaming up to do so, a spying eagle, a tracking puma and gangs of dogs and rattlesnakes working in unison. There's an odd stop-start quality to the narrative which one could perhaps charitably refer to as a kind of nightmare quality, there's an animal attack, some die, some escape, there's the hope of rescue, that hope is dashed, the animals attack again and so on. But while the emphasis is, as usual in a Girdler film, on propulsive action, there's also that recurring interest in oddly affecting monologues and some would-be philosophical digressions which tend to stick in the memory. As well as the conversation in Murphy's Bar, there's a later scene where

Santee, the Professor and Moore, by then outed as dying, discuss why they are in the predicament they're in:

Santee: No answer, no fair and no unfair.

Moore: Why don't we just kill ourselves and be done with it then?

Professor: Maybe we will. Maybe we already have.

The emphasis on canine antagonists in the later scenes may well be pragmatic – it's easier and presumably cheaper to train dogs than it is to train pumas or snakes – but the attack on the shack which end in the killings of Moore and the Professor is very intense with some frenzied cross-cutting. This sequence, like the earlier discussion in the hotel bar, owes an obvious debt to *The Birds* but it also displays a filmmaker displaying growing technical flair. The film also contains some of the most elaborate set-ups seen in Girdler's work until then including the evacuation of the town, a long caravan of army trucks and vehicles carrying their owners' possessions. There's nothing in *Day of the Animals* to equal the technical mastery and visceral attack sequences of Spielberg's take on the animal attack sub-genre (the latter is underrated as a director of sadistic action, the opening midnight encounter with the shark being more intense than any number of death scenes in more "adult-oriented" genre films). But the tone of Girdler's film is much bleaker than that of *Jaws* and the view of human frailty is pessimistic. And speaking of Chrissy, the unfortunate victim of Bruce the shark…

Monty Cox was the very accomplished trainer and also a stunt man, who worked with all of the animals and created a safe environment for cast and crew. His girlfriend was Suse Bakalini (sic.) who had done the opening scene being eaten by a shark while swimming naked in the movie "JAWS". All I remember was we were all smitten with Susie!" – Andrew Stevens.

Backlinie's presence was more just a referential nod however, as she was also a trained stunt woman who doubled for Day George in a couple of scenes.

Aside from the intensity of the animal attacks, there are some creepy scenes such as the moment Frank and the girl discover the isolated town, with another of those white picket fences and neatly manicured lawns serving as a contrast to the horrors (something which has in the intervening years become familiar through overuse). The scene where the soldiers in haz mat suits enter the town to find scattered corpses, both animal and human, feels like something out of George Romero while the notion of the threat simply dispersing is reminiscent of the studied anti-climax of H.G Wells's *War of the Worlds* (1897). The story is credited to the notorious Montoro but the notoriety wouldn't stop there. The screenplay was written by the husband-and-wife team of William L. Norton and Eleanor E. Norton. He was a TV writer who wrote a handful of macho action movies including *The Scalphunters* (1968) which starred Burt Lancaster, the John Wayne vehicle *Brannigan* and four films for Burt Reynolds. He also wrote *Big Bad Mama* (1974) for producer Roger Corman, another of the period gangster films churned out in the wake of *Bonnie and Clyde,* so Norton would not have been unfamiliar with the Girdler M.O. Eleanor was his second wife and *Day of the Animals* was her first feature credit (according to IMDb, she only wrote one other film). The Nortons moved to Ireland in the 1980s and, after becoming sympathetic to the cause of Irish Republicanism, attempted to smuggle American guns to the Irish National Liberation Army. The guns were intercepted and in August 1987, Bill Norton was sentenced to 4 years in prison, Eleanor got 3. After being released early they sought asylum in Nicaragua where Bill Norton shot and killed a man who broke into his house and tied the couple up. After spending time in Cuba and Mexico, the Nortons ended up back in California, where Bill died in 2010 and was survived by Eleanor. He requested that his ashes be scattered in Northern Ireland. A New York Times obituary would accurately sum him up as a "writer wilder than his movies" (Weber 2010), adding:

Mr. Norton was not one to take his oeuvre too seriously; on the day before he died, according to his son, Bill, a nurse asked if she would know the movies he wrote. "I don't think your I.Q. is low enough," Mr. Norton replied (Ibid.)

The lurid poster design, a whole menagerie of angry animals with that scene-stealing puma front and center, for once is no exaggeration. Similarly, the trailer is a viscerally exciting 31 seconds, shots of the characters followed by a rapidly-edited montage of animals accompanied by some full-throttle screams. For once, the voiceover is purely descriptive, rather than a breathless exaggeration, "What begins as a pleasant day of hiking in the woods becomes... The Day of the Animals".

The New York Times gave it another of those reviews that condemns the film while at the same time making it sound unmissable. Dubbing it, ""The Birds" recycled by an equal-opportunity employer with an eye more on shock than suspense", it goes on:

"Day of the Animals" offers pretty scenery, and some repulsive animal attacks. Despite its putative concern for the environment, it is calculated more to incite terror than to inspire restraint. This film has been rated PG ("Parental Guidance Suggested"). Animal and human savagery, the latter in the form of an attempted rape, are apparently the reasons (anon d.1977).

Like many Girdler films, a minor cult has sprung up around the film, largely made up of people who saw the film as children. As well as praising the animal action, one element in particular seems to appeal, as is seen on Letterboxd. One user, Joe, dubs the film "Day of Leslie Nielsen Taking Off His Shirt and Declaring War on God" while someone calling himself, Tony the Terror is even more hyperbolic:

A shirtless Leslie Nielsen attacks a bear with his bare hands. I SALD (sic.) A SHIRTLESS LESLIE NIELSEN ATTACKS A BEAR WITH HIS BARE HANDS. What more can you ask for?

What indeed? Novelist and Girdler fan Jim Knipfel accurately sums up the nihilistic appeal of Girdler's penultimate film:

There's no humor, no tension, nothing but an overwhelming sense of despair and rancor. Maybe that was the whole point, that humans are assholes who screwed up the environment and deserve what they get (Knipfel 2016).

Re-releasing the film a year later with a different title doubtless seems cynical these days but this was standard practice in the exploitation arena. In yet another example of the exploitation market eating itself, there was an Italian take on Girdler's penultimate film. Franco E. Prosperi's *Wild Beasts/Wild beasts – Belve feroci* (1984) deals with the escaped residents of Frankfurt Zoo terrorizing the city after drinking water contaminated with PCP. It manages to be wilder (pardon the pun) than the Girdler, especially the set piece with the tiger on the subway but also a lot less accomplished with murky photography and some woeful performances.

The ambiguity of the ostensibly happy ending of *Day of the Animals* is, once again, typical of both the director and the period. But things were changing. The bleakness and gloom which had been a mainstay of much of 1970s cinema was the product of various factors including the death of the hippy dream and Vietnam/the energy crisis/Watergate, the collapse of the Production Code, the influence of foreign auteur cinema on film school educated directors and a shift in audience demographics which meant audiences got younger and consequently more open to experimental cinema. In a short-lived period in Hollywood, bleak and gloomy was regarded as a kind of badge of artistic authenticity. As well as being very well-directed, so many of the films from this period – *The Godfather, The Exorcist, Taxi Driver*, the films of Altman, Kubrick, Polanski, even the blockbuster smash *Jaws* – were pretty dark fare. The Academy Awards of 1977 look, in retrospect, like a hint of things to come when the complex, adult-oriented likes of *Network* (1976), *All the President's Men* (1976), *Bound for Glory* (1976) and *Taxi Driver* were beaten by the feel-good *Rocky* (1976). That and the unprecedented success of *Star Wars* (1977) suggested audiences were hungry for a return to escapist good against evil narratives. Ever the pragmatist, Girdler found a way to blend occult horror with flashy Lucas-style thrills in what was to be his last film.

Chapter 10 - *The Manitou* (1978): Evil Does Not Die...It Waits...To Be Re-Born

Synopsis: We start with a dramatic Lalo Schifrin score over images of Native American masks and tribal art. Then there's a metallic crash and the screen is filled with X-rays of a skull. It belongs to Karen Tandy (Susan Strasberg), a patient in a San Francisco hospital with a large lump on her neck. It's growing at a rate of "7.3 mm per hour" although as she tells her doctors, Hughes (Jon Cedar) and McEvoy (Paul Mantee), it's only three days old. She adds how while it's not painful, "it moves sometimes, it almost shifts as if…well, as if someone were trying to turn over and get comfortable in bed". The doctors confer, suggesting it appears to be a fetus although this can't be possible.

Across town, we meet Harry Erskine (Tony Curtis), a fake medium who good naturedly bilks a series of elderly women by pretending to read their fortunes. It's clear he isn't a bad guy, partly by the diegetic flute music he plays during his readings, partly because of the twinkle in Curtis's eye. His clients are clearly moneyed, dressed in ridiculous feathered hats and overlong fur stoles and clearly meant to be foolish, with Mrs. Winconis (Jeanette Nolan) slightly troubled by Harry's prediction of "an attack of gas, probably something you ate" and visibly excited at the news she'll receive an obscene phone call. After getting her out the door with a meaningless "mystic motto" he can't get straight himself, his status as con artist is confirmed if not overstated, with him ripping off his robe and moustache (sticking the latter on the wall) and dancing round the apartment to disco music. Karen contacts Harry and they meet, taking a scenic walk around the city. Indeed, it's clear that Girdler is happy to be shooting in this most cinematic of cities, with repeated shots of Golden Gate Bridge and scenes in Golden Gate Park, Fisherman's Wharf and on cable cars. One could play a *Manitou* drinking game, taking a drink every time we hear the sound of a cable car bell. Harry and Karen are old flames who rekindle their romance back at his apartment. His playful attempt to read the Tarot (predictably) leads to Disaster, the Devil and Death. That night as they sleep by the open fire Karen repeats three words in her sleep, "pana witchy salatu". The next day, Karen checks into the hospital but during the operation, she wakes and Hughes is compelled by a mysterious force to cut into his own wrist with his scalpel. At his flat, Harry has another client and again, the Death card appears. The elderly Mrs. Hurst has an attack before starting to dance, chanting that same three-word incantation before floating out of the room and crashing down the stairs. Harry goes to see Hughes in his office, which is a remarkable example of set dressing, what with lots of bound medical tomes, framed certificates on the wall, a decanter of whisky and an enormous computer which foreshadows the climactic battle of the Manitous. Harry then visits his mentor, Amelia Crusoe (Stella Stevens) and her husband MacArthur (Hugh Corcoran) in their occult bookshop, the seaside setting of which inspires a visual flourish, the scene shot through an enormous metal propellor. Harry convinces Amelia to stage a séance in Karen's apartment which (again predictably) unleashes havoc, green lighting, that incantation and a ghostly head which emerges from the table (a very impressive effect). It climaxes with an explosion and a bolt of lightning which splits the table in two. The observation that the ghostly head was reminiscent of "a wooden Indian" along with Amelia's suggestion that the mysterious presence has "a vast knowledge of the occult… black magic" leads the trio to Dr. Snow (Burgess Meredith) an anthropologist and expert in Native American mythology (the trip to visit Snow in Sausalito allowing for yet more footage of the Golden Gate Bridge). Snow tells them about medicine men and their Manitous, or "immortal spirits" that can be reborn by impregnating a man, woman or child. He also translates that three-word incantation into "my death foretells my return". He suggests it would be "criminal" to destroy the reincarnated medicine man but Harry, thinking of Karen, isn't convinced. Back at the hospital, another attempt to operate on Karen goes wrong when a laser goes out of control and destroys the theater. She tells Harry and Hughes that the spirit within her is "in pain, it was the light" and the doctor works out that she's referring to the numerous x-rays she received. Snow's suggestion that they "fight fire with fire" leads Harry to John Singing Rock, a powerful medicine man who is initially reluctant to help "Mr. White Man":

Singing Rock: Would you do it if you were me?

Erskine: (Laughs) No, I guess I wouldn't.

But he agrees, in return for a donation to an Indian charity and some tobacco. The film then shifts to the hospital and the main setting, the virtually abandoned ward (we're told Karen is the only patient). The bland, generic set looks like something from a daytime soap about doctors so the horrors taking place have a jarring, disorienting quality. Singing Rock is freaked out to find he's dealing with Misquamacus, "the greatest medicine man of all". There's an odd moment when a nurse gives Harry some Alka Seltzer and it doesn't dissolve in water, presumably a sign of Misquamacus's growing power. While Harry – and we – are working out what this means, another nurse crashes through the door to Karen's room, covered in blood (we later find out he's been skinned). Great splashes of his blood cover the walls of her room while his body is left lying on the floor, covered with a blanket. Misquamacus emerges from the hideous hump on Karen's back and Singing Rock manages to put him to sleep. He also takes time to explain to Harry and Hughes how everything, even man-made things have Manitous (thus covering up a potential plot hole, they can't call the police because the medicine man might be able to control the Manitous in their guns). A nurse volunteering to stay in the room with the wounded Karen, the skinned corpse and the unresponsive medicine man stretches credibility to breaking point – and his actually falling asleep in there possibly snaps it in two – and he's awoken by his reanimated colleague. Misquamacus conjures up a reptilian god (which looks very like a transparent version of the Lizard Man from *Star Trek*) which attacks Hughes. When Harry and co. regroup in the doctor's office, he sees the computer and suggests using the Manitous of all the hospital's machines to launch an attack on the medicine man before he can summon the ominously-sounding Great Old One. Harry goes back to Karen's ward and exits the lift to find everything frozen, great heaps of ice piled up, icicles hanging from the roof and a nurse petrified, mid-gesture.

There's a sudden explosion, which causes the Nurse's head to snap off and go flying through a window (an eye-opening scene which isn't in the screenplay and seems to owe something to David Warner's spectacular exit from *The Omen* [1976]). Apparently the ice is courtesy of a demon known as the Star Beast. There's a real sense of bargain basement surrealism as we move from icy wasteland to space, with Karen's bed and the hysterically chuckling Misquamacus suspended among the stars (the music cue here sounds very like the *Star Trek* theme and it's hard to know whether it's accidental or an in-joke). The hospital machinery manifests its power in Karen and she rises up, nude but very tastefully lit, and fires bolts of light at the medicine man. There's a *2001: A Space Odyssey*-style light show and the lurking Great Old One is represented as a colorful optical effect. Karen's magic wins out and Misquamacus ends up a blackened scorch mark on the floor.

As Harry bids farewell to John Singing Rock, handing him his tobacco, he is informed that they may not have heard the last of the evil medicine man, his body may be dead but he isn't (thus leaving the way open for potential sequels). The film ends on an appropriately hokey note with more travelogue-style shots of San Francisco and an on-screen text.

Fact: Tokyo, Japan 1969. A fifteen-year-old boy developed what doctors thought was a tumor in his chest. The larger it grew the more uncharacteristic it appeared. Eventually it proved to be a human fetus.

This text appears at the start of the screenplay, which makes more sense although it may also be regarded as a spoiler.

Graham Masterton

It was in 1975 and *The Exorcist* had made a considerable impact. I had five days spare in between sex books so I spent them hammering out The Manitou, which was inspired by [his wife] Wiescka's pregnancy with our first son, mixed with a Native American legend which I remembered from *The Buffalo Bill Annual, 1955,* about manitous, the spirits that live in trees and rocks and wind and water and buffalo (Masterton 2014).

Born in 1946, Graham Masterton worked as a journalist and then moved on to the then-thriving world of soft-core men's magazines, editing *Mayfair* and the British edition of *Penthouse*. He's been incredibly prolific, having written sex manuals, crime stories, historical fiction and even a collaboration with William Burroughs (*Rules of Duel* [2010]) but Masterton is best-known for his horror novels. He's especially fond of conjuring demons specific to various nations and cultures, be it the Middle East (*Djinn* [1977]), ancient Egypt (*The Sphinx* [1978]), Japan (*Tengu* [1983]) or Nazi Germany (*The Devils of D-Day* [1979]). *The Manitou* may be his most famous novel, in large part because of Girdler's adaptation but it's only one of his Native American-inspired stories, there's also string of *Manitou* sequels and the unrelated *Charnel House* (1978). It's surprising that their haven't been more Masterton film adaptations, given his trademark memorable characterization, fast-pacing and plentiful sex and gore. *The Manitou* novel, reportedly written in five days (!) rattles along at a breathless pace. At times, it reads more like a screenplay, moving swiftly between striking set-pieces, so much so it makes you wonder if Girdler ever considered asking the author to adapt his own novel. It begins with a quote from H. P. Lovecraft:

On being ask'd what ye Daemon look'd like the antient (sic.) Wonder-Worker Misquamacus covered his face so that onlie ye Eyes look'd out and then gave a very curious and Circumstantiall (sic.) Relation, saying it was sometimes small and solid, like a Great Toad ye Bigness of many Ground-Hogs but sometimes big and cloudy, with no Shape, though with a face which had Serpents grown from it (Masterton 1976:6).

Indeed, the character of Misquamacus is borrowed from Lovecraft, who refers to a (fictional) book called *Of Evill (sic.) Sorceries Done in New-England of Daemons in No Humane Shape.* An "ancient Wonder-Worker" from the Wampanaug Tribe, he has the ability to be reborn after his death. Lovecraft wrote small fragments of the story (apparently, just over a thousand words) which was later turned into *The Lurker at the Threshold* (1945), a novel by August Derleth. Masterton takes this idea and transplants Misquamacus from 19th century New England to 1970s New York City (not San Francisco, one of the many differences between book and film). Indeed, the novel is very evocative in its wintry East Coast setting. Masterton's Erskine is young, in his early thirties and is presented as much less flashy and charismatic than Curtis's portrayal. Karen is a stranger and comes to him looking for psychic assistance (her aunt is one of Harry's clients). She's troubled by a frightening recurring dream of a galleon and instead of that three-word incantation, it's a few words of Dutch she – and the unfortunate Mrs. Winconis – are given to uttering. While the movie Karen is, as Snow puts it, "at the right place at the wrong time" in the novel her apartment is built on the site of an Indian village which was home to Misquamacus in life. The Dutch galleon is one of the medicine man's memories, a stark vision of the white invaders.

In a nice reflexive touch, Masterton's characters refer to *The Exorcist* not once but twice, the enormous success of which spawned a wave of occult horror which includes not only *Abby* but also the novel we're reading. In a stark example of one-upmanship, Dr. Snow refers to Blatty/Friedkin's demonic antagonist Pazuzu as nothing more terrifying than a mongrel dog" to an Indian (Masterton 1976: 72). Masterton performs a delicate balancing act between credibility and absurdity, although his characters often find themselves accepting the most bizarre of scenarios with little resistance:

I found a medium, Dr: Hughes, and we held a séance tonight in Karen´s apartment. There was some kind of manifestation – a face. All of us saw it. We´ve been checking through books on Indian history and stuff like that and we think it might be an Indian medicine man of the seventeenth century. According to one of these books – hold on – Indian medicine men ´if threatened, could destroy themselves by drinking blazing oil, and be reborn at any time or place in the future or the past by impregnating themselves into the body of a man, woman or animal.` Do you think that fits, Dr. Hughes? (Masterton 1976:64).

As a kind of justification, Erskine goes on to observe:

I´m always amazed how readily and quickly people will accept the occult and the supernatural, once the evidence is there in front of their eyes. Dr. Snow has probably read about medicine man reincarnation for years, without really believing it was possible, but as soon as someone had told him it had actually happened, he was ready to accept it without a qualm (Masterton 1976: 69).

The author´s consideration of Native American issues is more nuanced and considerably less stereotypical than those of the film. Whereas Girdler´s Misquamacus is an unambiguously evil creation with no justification given for his malevolence, Masterton´s medicine man is a monster with a cause. As Dr. Hughes observes:

The fascinating thing about America is that it was always supposed to be a brand new nation, free of oppression and free of guilt. But from the moment the white man settled here, there was a built-in time bomb of guilt. In the Declaration of Independence, there is even an attempt to gloss over this guilt, you remember? Jefferson wrote about the ´merciless Indian Savages, whose known rule of warfare is an undistinguished destruction of all ages, sexes and conditions. ` Right from the beginning, the Indian has not counted as an individual who is endowed by his Creator with those certain inalienable rights...This isn´t *our* land, Harry. This is the land we *stole*...I know we´ve all been talking about destroying this medicine man, and fighting him, but don't you feel some sympathy for him as well? (Masterton 1976: 79 – 80, emphasis in original).

Harry answers by saying he has sympathy for Karen but he admits to himself that:

In a strange way, Jack Hughes was right. I did feel something. There was a tiny part of my brain that wanted him to survive…I was terrified of his powers and his mastery of the occult, but at the same time he was like a mythical hero of legend, and to destroy him would mean destroying something of America's heritage. He was a lone survivor from our country's shameful past, and to kill him would be like grinding out the last spark of the spirit that had given the United States such a colorful and mystical background. He was the last representative of American magic. (Masterton 1976: 81)

Masterton's Singing Rock is very different to Michael Ansara, a short-haired, bespectacled man with a mohair suit and an investment business who looks "like an insurance salesman" (1976: 85). He's also not interested in charitable donations and tobacco so much as he is thousands of dollars, supplied by Karen's wealthy parents. While Girdler lets Amelia and McCarthy live, Masterton kills them off, burned to death by something called "lightning-that-sees". The description of the reborn medicine man is fairly close to that of the film:

His long black hair was flattened against his broad skull with oil and fluid. His eyes were stuck closed, and his coppery skin glistened with the fetid muck of his womb. His cheekbones were high and flat, and his prominent hooked nose was occluded with fetal fats. Strings of mucus hung from his lips and chin…his genitals were puffy and swollen, the same way that a boy child's are at birth, but there was dark pubic hair smeared against his scarred belly…And it was now that we saw what damage the X-rays had done to him. Instead of full muscular legs, his lower limbs both ended above the knee, in tiny deformed club feet, with pulpy dwarfish toes. Modern technology had crippled the medicine man in his womb (1976: 107 – 8).

The novel's medicine man has powers both much more subtle (so subtle they'd be virtually impossible to depict on film) and much more violent. At one point, in the besieged hospital, Harry feels strange, as if he's "breathing nitrous oxide at the dentist" and Singing Rock intervenes, telling him how Misquamacus "will do many strange things to your mind. He will try and make you feel like you do not really exist like he did and suicidal and desperately alone" (1976: 105 – 6). There's also an emphasis on smells including the scent of rotting fish when the sac is ripped open, which again, would be hard to pull off on screen. The re/birth sequence is also a lot messier, with blood, phlegm, and amniotic fluid. The Nurse in Karen's room isn't skinned but turned inside out, so the moment when he's reanimated is considerably more unpleasant and when the cops arrive, they are chopped up into frozen pieces by the medicine man's powers. Our protagonists work out that Misquamacus was frightened not of the guns or the god of the Dutch invaders but of their diseases, so they attempt to dose him with influenza before they enlist the aid of the technological Manitous (in this instance, a police computer). In the climactic scenes, Masterton seems to summon up Lovecraft, both in his description of the Great Old One as a kind of hideous squid and his depiction of the medicine man on the verge of triumph:

The room was thick with evil-smelling smoke, pouring ceaselessly from two fires which Misquamacus had lit in metal bowls, and placed on either side of his astral gateway. On the floor was marked out the most sinister and bizarre circle of figures that I had ever seen, all elaborately drawn and colored in what must have been the gore of Lieutenant Marino's police officers. There were strange goats and hideous creatures like enormous slugs, and naked women with loathsome beasts emerging from their wombs. Presiding over this circle, hunched and deformed, his dark body blurry with the smoke, was Misquamacus. But it was not Misquamacus himself that struck the greatest terror in us – it was what we could dimly perceive through the densest clouds of smoke – a boiling turmoil of sinister shadow that seemed to grow and grow through the gloom like a squid or some raw and massive confusion of snakes and beasts and monsters (1976: 167).

The most effective moment comes when Harry glimpses this vision of hell on earth and it transforms the novel from a farfetched story of a medicine man coming out of a woman's neck into a slice of existential evil:

What was so terrifying was that I *recognized* the Great Old One – I recognized how close he had always been to me. He was the fright of strange shapes in wallpaper and drapes; the terror of faces that appear in the grain of wooden wardrobes; the fear of darkened stairs or curious and half-seen reflections in mirrors and windows. Here, in the writhing shape of the Great Old One, I discovered where all my long-buried fears and anxieties had come from. Every time you hear disembodied breathing in your bedroom at night; every time the clothes you have carelessly left on your chair seem to take the form of a sinister and monkish figure; every time you think you hear footsteps behind you as you climb the stairs – *it is the evil presence of the Great Old One, straining malevolently at the locks and seals which keep him on the other side* (1976: 166; emphasis in original).

Reading that, it isn't hard to see why Masterton, a self-confessed admirer of the film, had problems with Girdler's intergalactic ending. In the closing pages of the novel the evil that Misquamacus embodies is repackaged as the kind of unease and terror that we can all relate to and this continues right up to the last line. Harry visits the seemingly rejuvenated Karen in the country house of her parents and as he's about to leave, she says "De boot, mijnheer", the same Dutch phrase spoken earlier by his possessed client. When questioned, she claims to have said merely, "Be good, my dear" and the sense of lingering disquiet this creates is familiar from Girdler's other horror films, although conspicuously absent from his take on *The Manitou.*

I was flying to London to oversee the scoring for 'Day of the Animals'. At the airport in New York, I bought a paperback copy of 'Manitou'. I read it straight through and knew it was a great film. I got off the plane in London and called one of my associates in Hollywood and said, "Sell the cars, hock the office equipment, do anything you have to do to get it, but get it today." (Girdler in Breen 2000-1).

It really isn't hard to see why Masterton's novel would appeal to the director, the vaguely absurd set-up played totally straight, the bizarre imagery and its commercial appeal, melding as it does the supernatural hi-jinks of *The Exorcist* with the cosmic good against evil narrative of *Star Wars*. Masterton was familiar with the director's work:

I was aware of Bill Girdler's films before he approached my agent Stephanie Bennett to develop The Manitou. I had seen Grizzly and Day of the Animals and I was aware of his Blaxploitation movies.

He also liked Girdler's enthusiasm for the Native American aspects of the story:

He told me that he was immediately attracted to *The Manitou* because it concerned Native American mythology and hardly anybody had written about that in a horror story before, apart from Algernon Blackwood's story about the Wendigo. Actually that was the USP of *The Manitou* and that was what led to its selling nearly half a million copies in the first six months of its publication. What Bill said he liked about it so much was that it wasn't about vampires or werewolves or zombies or any of the usual horror tropes. In fact Sitting Bull's grand-daughter took me to lunch at the Russian Tea Room in New York and gave me a framed picture of Sitting Bull because the Sioux were so pleased by the story – Graham Masterton.

While the "Native American burial ground" is a genre staple, having featured in the likes of *The Amityville Horror* (1979), *The Shining* (1980) and *Poltergeist* (1982), it's been comprehensively debunked by Jesse Wente in the documentary *Woodlands Dark and Days Bewitched* (2021). For a long time Indigenous American mythology was largely ignored in the horror genre, with a few notable exceptions such as the Blackwood story noted by Masterton and *The Werewolf* [1913]. This 18-minute short about a Navajo witch and her daughter who transforms into a wolf was the first screen treatment of lycanthropy (sadly, the film is now thought lost). But the film version of Masterton's novel was part of a mini-wave of Native American-themed genre films along with *Nightwing* (1979), another eco horror, the time round starring a caveful of vampire bats and *Wolfen* (1980), another werewolf story. Famously, when the studio asked Girdler if he had a script for what would be his first adaptation, he lied and said yes, suggesting that he really was getting used to flying by the seat of his pants. But then if *Sheba Baby* could be put together in a day... This led to a mad scramble to come up with a screenplay. With time ticking away, Girdler approached screenwriter Thomas Pope, who realized right away the script needed a lot of work. Whereas the majority of the earlier Girdler scripts were thrown together by committee, with various people pitching in, Pope had studied screenwriting and had strong ideas about structure and character. He would go on to work on projects for Coppola, Ridley Scott and David Fincher and although today he makes no great claims for *The Manitou*, it's clear he took his job seriously. Pope liked the director, at least at first but wasn't impressed by his production partner, the actor Jon Cedar:

He and Jon Cedar, his old and not too bright would-be actor buddy, had written a draft of their own, which was no good, and they knew they needed a rewrite. Bill was only partnered with Jon, so far as I could see, because Jon's wife, Barbara, ran a typing shop (really, a sort of mini-factory) on Santa Monica and Fairfax (Barbara's Place – we satisfy!) where, literally fifty women sat in a large room, all of them typing away on IBM Selectrics on scripts that needed re-writes, new drafts, whatever. Before computers, everything was typed, and Barbara's was the place that many of the studios sent their scripts for a quickie re-type. Messengers from the studios came and went like clockwork, picking up and dropping off scripts – Thomas Pope.

Pope didn´t actually read the source novel, possibly because there was no time to do so. Comparing what was supposed to be the final draft of the screenplay dated February 26th 1977 against the finished film, it´s clear changes were being made during production but then this is more often the case than not, any number of things can lead to things being changed during the shoot. On the first page, there´s that Lovecraft quote as a foreword, something which was presumably too arty and obscure to make it into the film. The credits play over a vaguely abstract sequence of Karen being X-rayed which comes across like something out of the previous year´s *Demon Seed*:

And Karen is alone with the machine. She stares up into its cyclops eye as, almost sexually, it moves down on her. And the X-ray eye grows bigger and bigger IN THE FRAME, nearly covering helpless Karen. The black of the cyclops X-ray eye begins FILLING THE FRAME until the entire SCREEN is brought into total darkness and we…

END TITLES.

A lot of Masterton's dialogue made its way into the script verbatim, far more than ends up in the finished film, presumably from one or more of the Girdler/Cedar drafts. Harry here is younger still, aged 28. The scenic walk he takes with Karen is not only scripted, it's even more scenic with the ex-lovers taking a ferry across the Bay. Her dreams of disease are graphically described ("black pus, blood…and everyone dying…horribly dying") and she also dreams of Misquamacus's suicide through drinking blazing oil (although it's not clear this is what she's doing). The invaders in the screenplay aren't the Dutch arriving in what would become New Amsterdam but the English led by Francis Drake, bringing with them a form of cholera, a change presumably necessitated by the shift in location from the East to the West coast. The screenplay delves much deeper into the mythology of the Native Americans courtesy of Dr. Snow and while it's interesting background, it's easy to see why Girdler cut back on it – he's making a spectacular horror fantasy after all. It's also interesting to see where the director added his own idiosyncratic or sensational touches (a prominently placed DC comic, the decapitated nurse).

There's an effectively oppressive quality to the screenplay's conflict in the hospital, stripped as it is of Girdler's cosmic sequence and Masterton's cops and reporters. The script's notion of the hospital technology being used works better than the police computer of the novel and, anticipating the film, it's channelled through the revived Karen. Interestingly, even as late as the final draft, the intergalactic finale is not present (suggesting perhaps that Girdler hadn't yet seen *Star Wars*). Instead, the ending is close to the Lovecraftian stylings of the novel, with the half-glimpsed, tentacled Great Old One. Although we remain resolutely earthbound, there is the potential for some extravagant special effects:

Suddenly, Karen's body, on the bed, starts to glow. Softly at first but pulsating. She moves, the opening on her back seals closed… She starts to rise to a sitting position, the pulsating glow growing stronger and brighter with each pulse. She raises her hands towards

Misquamacus, then opens her eyes. Negative…bottomless…a universe behind them…She opens her mouth and lets out a roar,,,An EXPLOSION, accompanied by a phosphorescent flash that almost seems to tear the building apart around Harry…The room is blotted out by a dazzling array of incandescent grid shapes – tier after tier of brilliant circuitry – crawling with white and blue sparks and shimmering with its own blinding symmetry. Misqaumacus is knocked to the floor, his body charred, blackened and bloody,

The ending of the screenplay is, *pace* Masterton, disquieting as Harry visits the seemingly cured Karen in her hospital room:

Harry approaches the door to the room and US, walking INTO A CLOSEUP. Karen watches him go with a smile. Then:

KAREN
(quietly)
Pana…wich-ee…salitu.

HARRY freezes in his tracks. What did she say?

FREEZE FRAME.

ANOTHER ANGLE

Another FROZEN FRAME of Harry from the side.

ANOTHER ANGLE

Another FREEZE FRAME of Harry's back…
ANOTHER ANGLE

A WIDER FREEZE FRAME of the whole room INCLUDING Karen on the bed and Harry at the door.

EXT. HOSPITAL – DAY

A CLOSE-UP on a window on the eighth floor. We SLOWLY ZOOM OUT to an EXTREME WIDE SHOT of the city of San Francisco…

FADE OUT.

In a sign of just how far Girdler had come, the shooting schedule was a comparatively leisurely ten weeks, starting in May 1977 and carrying on through the summer. The decision to move location from New York to San Francisco may have been motivated by cost (the interiors were shot at CBS in Hollywood) but for Girdler, speaking in 1977, it was his choice, "San Francisco is moody in a way New York isn't, the fog, the architecture, very Mediterranean" (Frentzen 1978).

There are a couple of ways to regard Tony Curtis's involvement in the film. He was by far the biggest name the director had worked with to date, a genuine star from Hollywood's Golden Age. Born in the Bronx in 1925, Curtis started his career as a Universal contract player in his early mid-20s. He was startlingly handsome as a young man and made a string of lightweight films such as *The Prince Who Was a Thief* (1951) and *Son of Ali Baba* (1952) where he was required to do little more than be athletic and look good in tights. But he more than proved himself with impressive turns in *Sweet Smell of Success* (1957) and *Some Like It Hot* (1959). As his looks started to fade and his career waned, he was very creepy as Albert De Salvo in Richard Fleischer's flashy *The Boston Strangler* (1968). The TV show *The Persuaders* (1971) which teamed Curtis with Roger Moore is still fondly remembered by British TV viewers of a certain age, especially the evocative John Barry score but it never took off in the US. He was good as part of a very starry cast in *The Last Tycoon* (1976) but the films he made the same year as *The Manitou*, *Sextette* (1978) and *The Bad News Bears Go to Japan* (1978) were far from his best. Off-screen, he was freebasing cocaine and drinking heavily. But this was also a period, post-*The Exorcist*, when big stars were unafraid to make horror films. Gregory Peck and Lee Remick were the adopted parents of the antichrist in *The Omen*, Richard Burton was a bedbound telekinetic author in *The Medusa Touch* (1978) and Kirk Douglas would pop up in both *The Fury* ([1978], another tale of telekinesis) and the lurid Italian *Omen* rip-off, *Holocaust 2000* (1980). Even with his star somewhat dimmed, Curtis's involvement did a lot to raise the profile of the project. On one occasion, screenwriter Pope was on set watching Curtis work and, contrary to the rumors about the actor being messed up on drugs (some of which came from Curtis himself) his performance was impressive:

Bill gave Tony lots of directions. It was only Tony making a phone call, and yet I was amazed at how adept Curtis was at listening and taking all of Bill's advice – Curtis did it all, line by line, direction by direction (turn left on this line, hang up on this line, turn right as you leave, etc.) on the first take. I've rarely learned so much in so short a time. Amazing.

Curtis certainly seems to be having a good time, switching effortlessly from mystic in an embroidered cloak and stick-on moustache and dancing around his apartment drinking beer from a wine glass after he's been paid. Masterton's Erskine may be a con man but he does seem to believe in the supernatural, so much so he reads his own Tarot to try and make sense of what's going on. Sometimes Curtis's playful manner doesn't work and it does stretch credibility that anyone would be making lame jokes when the future of the world is at stake from The Great Old One:

Singing Rock: Here (handing Harry a charm).

Erskine: What's this for?

SR: Protection.

E: Oh, I thought it was seasoning.

But in a weird way, Harry's befuddlement at being in such a situation can be seen as mirroring the actor's feelings at being cast in such a goofy movie. Aside from Curtis, the rest of the cast was typical for Girdler, a combination of half-remembered performers from yesteryear, some interesting newer talent and some familiar faces. Susan Strasberg, the daughter of renowned acting coach Lee plays Karen Tandy, the unfortunate host for the reborn Misquamacus. Unsurprisingly given her showbiz background, she made an impact as a teenager, appearing in *Picnic* (1955) and originating the title role in *The Diary of Anne Frank* on Broadway. In the late 60s, married to the cult actor Christopher Jones, she appeared in a string of counterculture movies including *The Trip* and *Psych Out* (1968). The 70s saw her working mainly in TV and post-*The Manitou*, she made some low-profile genre films and turned to writing as acting offers dried up. Among the veterans, Burgess Meredith steals the show as the eccentric anthropologist Dr. Snow and the actor's contribution was key to the characterization:

I do recall that Bill allowed the actors to play with the script, so that Burgess Meredith's jokey-curmudgeonly interpretation was his alone and helps the script a lot - Pope.

Meredith had an acclaimed theatrical career and appeared in some high-profile films such as *Of Mice and Men* (1939) and *The Story of GI Joe* (1945) as well as a number of Otto Preminger projects. But he also had serious cult credentials, appearing in one of the most fondly remembered episodes of *The Twilight Zone* (1959 – 64), *Time Enough at Last* (1959) and playing The Penguin in the *Batman* TV show (1966 – 68). In the 70s, he moved effortlessly from prestige projects like *Day of the Locust* (1975) and *Rocky* to some interesting off-beat horror films including *Burnt Offerings* (1976) and *The Sentinel* (1977). A large part of his appeal to genre filmmakers was his remarkable voice, cracked and extremely expressive.

Stella Stevens, who plays Amelia Crusoe, the retired psychic who taught Erskine all he knows, was probably best-known for her role in *The Poseidon Adventure* (1972), although she's excellent in Sam Peckinpah's underrated *The Ballad of Cable Hogue* (1970). Her son, Andrew Stevens had played one of the leads in *Day of the Animals*. The fact that Erskine's clientele is made up exclusively of elderly women gave the director the chance to cast some semi-famous performers from old Hollywood. Anne Sothern, who had her own TV show in the late 1950s is Mrs, Karmann, Karen´s aunt and séance attendee, Jeanette Nolan, who played Lady Macbeth opposite Orson Welles in 1948 is the neurotic Mrs. Winconis and Lurene Tuttle, a prolific radio performer who had appeared in *Psycho*, played the unfortunate Mrs. Herz, who is thrown down the stairs. Fresh from *Day of the Animals*, Cedar, Paul Mantee and Michael Ansara also crop up here, the latter as John Singing Rock, the rival medicine man. The actor was actually of Lebanese descent and born in Syria but appeared frequently as Native Americans in Westerns. According to Pope, the character was initially underwritten:

I especially remember going into (sic.) Bill in the middle of the rewrites and saying that Singing Rock, the Indian Medicine Man, just shows up out of nowhere —where did he come from, why is he working for Tony, what sort of a guy is he? I suggested that Tony fly out to South Dakota where real Indians live, and hire Singing Rock there – oh, and give him a first name, how about John? Bill said go ahead and, in a furious half an hour, or less, I wrote the South Dakota scene, maybe the best scene in the movie (for whatever that's worth) and which was shot in Southern California somewhere. I remember meeting on the set with Michael Ansara, who played Singing Rock, who praised me for the scene ("It's well written!") – I've rarely felt so proud -Pope.

There´s also a brief appearance by Girdler staple Charles Kissinger as an anesthesiologist. I wonder if he ever pondered the fact that if the film had been made in Kentucky, he´d be playing Harry Erskine?

The odd streak of black humor running through the project appealed to Masterton:

We shared a similar sense of humour and I was pleased when -- in the film -- he faithfully mirrored the humorous elements that were in the book…What did impress me about Bill's direction was the great cast he managed to assemble, and the performances that he got out of them. Although the premise of the story is quite absurd ('A foetus...on her neck??') he got them to play their parts completely straight, which made the absurdity quite convincing - Masterton.

Apart from the bizarre premise, both ludicrous and repulsive, the film's reputation rests largely on the strange mix of tones. It starts with a flat, almost TV movie feel vaguely reminiscent of Larry Cohen's *It's Alive* (1976), another film which manages to be unsettling despite a pretty silly premise but the introduction of the Erskine character lightens the mood considerably. As noted throughout, even at his most violent and whacky, there's a sort of sweetness about the director's work, unlike a lot of 1970s horror directors:

There is a certain joy in watching a Girdler film, something that's hard to describe. Especially since none of his films were comedies or family films. He dealt with straight up horror/action films...not a lot of joy in his scripts. But there is a certain exuberance in all of his work, it's evident that he was enjoying all of his time behind the camera & his actors/crew enjoyed working for him (Mr. Fright 2011).

The move away from the shock and gore of the novel was a deliberate choice made by Girdler, as he told Jeffrey Frentzen of *Cinefantastique* in an interview which would be published after his death:

Graham's book went to extremes that I did not wish to deal with...Much of the gore in the book has been eliminated. We had 2 choices in making the film. We could have made a drive-in shocker of immense proportions or a class production. The story could have been done either way. I wanted to get away from the kind of films I'd been doing up until that point (Frentzen 1978).

As well as the toned-down gore, there's some added romance in the form of the rekindled affair between Harry and Karen. It's handled delicately, although younger viewers may be startled by a Hollywood film which features a sexual relationship between mature characters, Curtis being in his early fifties, Strasberg thirteen years younger. The fact that he's a fair bit older than her indicate some things at least haven't changed. The love scenes also came from Pope:

Most of the work I did was cuts – the script had all of the talkiness of an amateur script – and I had to cut and cut. But I also recall inventing a number of scenes – the falling-in-love scenes between the hero (Tony Curtis) and the pregnant heroine (Susan Strasberg), staged in Golden Gate Park (I told you, they had a budget). I recall writing the love scene to be spoken slowly, lovingly, meaningfully, and was pole-axed to see it on the screen spoken quick, efficiently, and too fast for my intention – the thing was, the actor's interpretation worked better than my own, more pompous reading-in-my-head, and I learned a great lesson that day that lines can be written one way, and spoken another, and sometimes for the better.

From this unusually warm set-up, the film takes a turn into apocalyptic occult territory and ends up as a slice of space-bound science fiction. For most of the running time, the film veers between outright horror and black comedy. A good example of the latter is that early sequence when Cedar's doctor and Mantee's administrator have a discussion about Karen's tumor while in the background there a large wall chart illustrating pregnancy "From Egg to Birth" (a scene staged exactly as it is in the screenplay). Even so, the climactic spill over into sheer lunacy comes as a surprise. Indeed, "batshit" is a word that turns up often in fan's responses to the film. During the visit to Doctor Snow, MacArthur finds a DC *House of Mystery* comic lying around and flicks through it and this seemingly trivial incident is telling. The film resembles nothing so much as a comic book, lurid, shifting genres and sometimes cartoonish. There are also some er, homages to other films, not only the oft-noted *2001* and *Star Wars* space imagery but also visual references to better-known occult horror. For example, Girdler recycles a steal from *The Exorcist* which also turns up in *Abby*, a distorted female scream which acts as a bridge between scenes.

These days, the special effects look rather crude, especially the scenes where the hospital is frozen and filled with obviously plaster icicles, and I was not mad about the *Star Wars*y climax that appears to be in space. But of course *Star Wars* had just come out then, and Bill was very impressed by it - Masterton

Before things go *totally* batshit, the scenes in the hospital room are claustrophobic and imaginatively staged. The re/birth is effectively hideous, the sac stretching until it tears, an arm emerges from it and the creature itself is a monstrous thing, green-eyed, excessively-muscled, shrunken and covered in slime. The way Girdler tells it, he again went out of his way to avoid grossing out the audience, pointing out "there is no blood, oozing fluid or ripping flesh. The way it was done, complimented by Lalo Schifrin's score, achieves an ethereal mood" (Frentzen 1978). The reborn Misquamacus is played by two different actors, Felix Zilla, a circus performer best known for playing Cousin It in *The Addams Family* TV series (1964 – 66) and Joe Gieb in his screen debut.

One problem with the film is that ideas which read well in a novel or screenplay can he hard to realize on screen when you have a limited budget. Stanley Kubrick noted how, "if it can be written, or thought, it can be filmed" (in Nordern 1968) but then as someone who graduated from low-budget features early, he *could* say that. A good example of these limitations are the scenes in the frozen hospital. They're very spooky, with the immobile Nurse a particularly nice touch but the effect is undercut, as Masterton notes, by poor set dressing. There's an interesting echo here of *The Exorcist,* where the characters breath becomes visible as the temperature in Regan's room plunges and for once, Girdler manages to one-up Friedkin! In much the same way, the hospital room being relocated in space is also a very striking image but again, the budget isn't up to it. Although the scene where the room appears to be shaking is clearly a step up from the hand vibrators on the camera in *Abby*, there's a real physicality to it.

Girdler died in the January so never got to see the reaction to his most high-profile film, which was released at the end of April. While the trailer manages to pack in most of the eye-popping scenes in two and a half minutes, the poster design was, given such a sensational story, curiously underwhelming (especially when compared to that iconic *Grizzly* poster). The black and white image of a bed with a spooky face above a cloud of glowing smoke may be another nod to *The Exorcist* with its iconic poster image but in the end it didn't matter, Girdler's film was a hit. The initial critical response was mixed – but how could it not be when it came to a film about a medicine man growing on a woman's neck in late 1970s San Francisco? The critic Derek Adams comes closer that most in summing up the delirious mish mash of styles on display:

The special effects are superb, easy winners in an engaging inter-denominational free-for-all that blends Marvel Comics' Doctor Strange with Corman's *The Raven* (Adams 1977).

The critical reception has, over time, become much more favorable. As with both *Grizzly* and *Day of the Animals*, this is largely down to viewers who saw the film – or even just the trailers – as kids and found it (pardon the pun) bewitching and/or terrifying. There's also a feeling that its defiant weirdness is something to be treasured at a time when so many horror films are cookie-cutter bland ghost stories or bloodless remakes. As Jeffrey M. Anderson notes, "Even if the story becomes totally absurd, it has more in the way of creativity than most modern horror remakes" (2007).

Clearly, *The Manitou* is absurd, insane, and, yeah, kind of awful, but there's nevertheless a high watchability factor in checking out all these thespians intensely furrowing their brows and delivering their dialogue without breaking out in laughter (honestly, I never thought Curtis had this much professionalism in him) (Brunson 2019).

As one would expect of a novelist, Jim Knipfel accurately conveys the appeal of Girdler's final film for many:

While there are undeniable reminders of **The Exorcist** at the core of **The Manitou**, it's far more twisted than your typical knockoff. Trying to look at the film as a coherent whole is difficult, if only because the tone is so fluid and hard to pinpoint. It's fast and bright and occasionally funny (sometimes intentionally so), while at turns it's also dark, surreal, deeply disturbing, and just plain disgusting. Looking at the film straight on from beginning to end, no, it's a bit like watching a gas explosion in a mine filled with clowns. But if you look at it instead in terms of individual scenes and images and line readings and cameos, it's hard to forget (Knipfel 2017).

Masterton and Girdler had talked about adapting another of the writer's novels, *Djinn* (1977) which would've again starred Curtis as Erskine. Girdler had expressed concern that it would be hard to create a convincing tornado (the cow-whirling computer-generated likes of *Twister* [1996] were, of course, decades away). But shortly after, thirty miles outside Manila, an inexperienced helicopter pilot tried to fly beneath some power lines and put a sudden, violent stop to the fast times and great promise of Bill Girdler.

January 21st 1978

It was a Saturday. Reports differ as to what Girdler was doing back in Manila. Most accounts suggest he was scouting locations for his next feature, a space opera called *The Overlords*. But other sources have claimed the director was actually helping out on another film about the drug trade in the Philippines to be made by his traveling companion, the British producer Patrick Alan Kelly (no relation to the director's brother-in-law). Also along for the ride was Filipino film exec Dennis Lovan and the pilot was a young man called Jess Garcia. The accident happened at 4pm local time, the helicopter crashing in the jungle and exploding. All of the passengers were burned beyond recognition. Girdler's friend and frequent collaborator Joe Schulten told a moving story about the aftermath of the crash to Patti Breen:

Billy always wore his late father's watch as well as some family jewelry…Some villagers came across the crash scene and removed all the valuables from the victims. Pat Kelly went out to all the street markets, and eventually tracked down Billy's things to bring back home. He really cared about Billy (in Breen 2000-1).

But this contradicts the newspaper reports (including *The Courier-Journal*) that the bodies, which were burned beyond recognition, were identified by their jewelry. From Louisville to the jungle outside Manila via Hollywood. *The Manitou* opened three months later.

Chapter 11 - Roads Not Taken

It's always tempting to ask "what if" about any artists who die young. We have some ideas of the way William Girdler wanted his career to go, though. If, as expected he'd go on to higher-profile projects in the wake of *The Manitou*, he had no desire to abandon the kind of low-budget genre films that had made his name. According to Hugh Smith, after he reconciled with the director, they talked about collaborating on a low-budget film "about a mysterious serial killer back East" with Girdler producing and Smith writing and directing (see Breen 2000-1).

Graham Masterton too imagined further collaborations with the director, telling me that their "conversations were very creative and we were very much on the same wavelength. I believe that if he had lived we would have made many more movies together".

We know a little about *The Overlords*, a science fiction/fantasy written by screenwriter Harry Kleiner, whose previous credits included *Fantastic Voyage* (1966) and *Bullitt* (1968). Despite Girdler's protestations that "it is not a Star Wars rip-off" (Frentzen 1978), it seems to have been to Lucas's film what *Grizzly* was to *Jaws*, at least based on the teaser poster. Billed as "the most thought provoking time traveling adventure between man and those worlds beyond our universe" the poster features various generic images including suspended astronauts, spaceships, blasting lasers and aliens with a star-dotted backdrop. The project didn't end with Girdler's death and it was repackaged as a vehicle for Marvin Chomsky but ultimately it never happened.

The director also worked with *Manitou* screenwriter Thomas Pope on a number of potential projects and reading through the treatments they came up with offers a fascinating insight into what might have been.

Unmade Girdler

I'm certain that one or more of these treatments would have been made had Bill survived. You can almost chart out what directions Bill's career probably would have taken had he lived. And, very possibly, my own career. Ah, the alternative paths we all might have taken – Thomas Pope.

All of the treatments were written by Pope with Girdler sharing the story credit. As the screenwriter put it, "I turned out treatment after treatment for Bill…he supplied the ideas…and I supplied the words, typed out at a furious pace".

Knights of Glory.

This project was inspired by an image which came to Girdler in a hotel room "of the Magnificent Seven as knights in armor" (which would, of course, align the project more with Akira Kurosawa's *The Seven Samurai* [1954] rather than the Western remake). He was so pleased with the idea, he "whooped with joy, jumped up and down and felt like a hero". A lavishly mounted action film set in Medieval England, it's very different in scope and tone to the usual Girdler project and a good indication of how ambitious his plans were. The characters were mainly borrowed from TL White's *The Once and Future King* (1958) and they're broadly drawn, a stylishly-dressed, womanizing French bowman, a drunken Irish knight, a massive Viking. The action takes place some years after the fall of Camelot, which is now just a shell of its former self. Arthur, now in his sixties and Merlin, twenty years older, are relics of a former age:

They seemed like old, shrivelled up ladies, cackling and gossiping and waiting to die. White haired, petty, shrunken.

The action follows the Kurosawa/Sturges template very closely and there are regular bouts of action. There are hints of the squalor and barbarism of the later *Excalibur* (1981) but this is largely an uncomplicated Manichean struggle between the titular Knights and Mordred, Arthur's bastard son. A striking visual flourish would've been the blue steel swords forged from a meteor, or as the script puts it, "star's flesh". The project is a curiously old-fashioned one – and the setting very far from downtown Louisville – but there's a nostalgic sweetness about it which perhaps indicates the influence of George Lucas.

Last of the White House.

This is another fairly atypical idea, although the political paranoia of *Project:Kill* can perhaps be seen as a distant cousin. Like the earlier film, it's clearly a response to Watergate, Nixon and Liddy are name-checked and a *Washington Post* reporter has a key role in the narrative although given recent events in the US, the theme of a psychologically unstable, maybe even insane President seems oddly timely. The President in question is Matthew Harrison Tyler:

Tall, well-bred and educated, athletic, eloquent. Two Pulitzer Prizes, one for Literature, the other for History. Rhodes Scholar. Olympic Champion. Congressman. Senator. He even looked like a President.

As if that wasn't enough, he also has a 71% approval rating. His vice-president is Wendell Gordy from Louisiana, described as a "good ole boy", compared to Huey Long and nicknamed "the Bassett Hound". When a series of knife murders are committed – a couple in the White House itself – Gordy starts to suspect the President is the killer. The ending offers up a bizarre twist – Gordy is the real killer and he becomes President after shooting Tyler – while at the same time hinting at the possible restoration of order, Tyler's comatose widow knows the truth and her condition is improving. It's a pulpy thriller, light on credibility but full of twists and turns and it isn't hard to see why such a project would appeal to Girdler the Hitchcock fan. There's a real charge in presenting some gory slasher sequences in such incongruous surroundings and the glossy, overplotted mayhem anticipates the kind of "murder among the idle rich" vehicles that screenwriter Joe Eszterhas would turn out in the 1980s and 1990s (*Jagged Edge* [1987], *Basic Instinct* [1991]) while the twist ending seems like something from a particularly fevered

Brian De Palma film. Like all of these unmade projects, the scope is way beyond any previous Girdler film, yet another example of the director wanting to exploit his higher profile on the back of *The Manitou.*

Tooth and Claw **aka** *The Deadly Jungle* **(1978).**

This is maybe the most obviously Girdler-esque of the unmade projects, an eco-horror film in the vein of *Day of the Animals*, with which it shares a thematic conceit, animals banding together to seek revenge on mankind:

One thing of which there's no question: Mankind rules the world. Mankind has the finest technologies, the greatest intellects, the best organization. All of the animals acknowledge that. All of the birds, the reptiles, the insects: there isn't a creature alive that doesn't know Man is the Master.

And yet…What if?

What if that surprisingly delicate balance were broken? What if all the animals of all the breeds of all the species were to mass together? Animals so outnumber us that their sheer mass alone could crush us. And it could happen (emphasis in original)…it could happen as sure as God invented terror. What if, unconcerned for their own lives, the animals rush at us, moving fearlessly, inexorably forward? What then? What then, indeed.

This time, it's a plane full of nerve gas that crashes in an African waterhole rather than depleted ozone and instead of a disparate collection of hikers, it's the privileged members of the exclusive Safari Club. There's an element of class war here with various vaguely stereotypical representatives of what we'd now refer to as the 1%, a Japanese electronics tycoon who just wants to talk business and his horny wife, the Frenchman who plays Chopin on the piano, the British Viscount who knocks back endless Martinis and so on. The set-up is an excuse to string together a series of exciting set-pieces – an elephant crashing into a helicopter – and that slasher movie-ish emphasis, familiar from other Girdler films, on who will die and how. So the Viscount is attacked by birds and set on fire before he falls off a balcony and there's a couple of deaths by python. The best sequence has a land rover fleeing a rhino and landing in water. There's a moment of light relief – before the car starts to fill up with water and piranhas, which eat the occupants. There's also a last-minute supernatural twist which posits that alongside the serum, the animals are attacking the Safari Club because a witch doctor who sought to control them is buried beneath it.

The Final Game.

This is, as Pope freely admits, yet another version ("a total rip-off") of the much-filmed Richard Connell story, *The Most Dangerous Game* (1924). The screenwriter wryly suggested that of the unmade projects, "this deserves the most to be made, because it is so commercial and also the least to be made, because it is such a blatant rip-off". In truth, this project, another jungle adventure/body count tale which shares a number of thematic concerns with *Tooth and Claw* is more interesting than Pope makes it sound. It has another glamorous elite institution, this time the International Club for high-flying industrialists and it also takes place largely in Kinshasa. There's another multi-cultural cast (this time round the Japanese is a "motorcycle magnet" and the Frenchman is a "steel baron") and Girdler and Pope even reuse the names of the central duo, Ashland and Candice. The similarities between the two projects are indeed so marked as to suggest either one went nowhere and elements were recycled or there was a plan to shoot both films back-to-back. Both stories feature an elephant attacking a helicopter, an action set piece that presumably could be used more than once (and there's an unsettling aspect to the imagery of the trashed chopper, given that neither project saw the light because of a helicopter accident). The story of a disparate group playing a game in the jungle that turns deadly can clearly be read as social satire:

It was a game, only that. A break from the abstract struggles of corporate power. A break from the struggles in Board Rooms or in the Gaming Rooms of the CLUB (emphasis in original) to a real struggle, a struggle with real terrors. It was to be another game – merely that – only a game more real.

The idea of comfortably-off white collar workers fighting for their lives has echoes of *Deliverance* as well as the transformation of Leslie Nielsen's ad exec into a killer in *Day of the Animals* and it's still being used today (the office drones/would-be killers of *Hostel 2* [2007] and the deadly office politics of *The Belko Experiment* [2016]). As well as the man-made hazards the group encounter, such as deadly traps and explosions cooked up by mercenaries, there's the traditional animal attacks, from a pit of snakes to a tiger attack. This time the catalyst isn't ozone depletion or spilled serum but "*sunumi*", a kind of yellow fever which affects wildlife.

To date, these films remain unmade and the relationship between Girdler and Pope soured after the screenwriter felt snubbed by the director:

I thought of Bill as a sort of friend, and we talked of other projects but I drifted rather sadly and angrily away from him soon after The Manitou came out and started making money. He and Melvin Gordy formed a partnership and took an office in Studio City. I remember stopping by one day to say hello, and saw him freeze me with a condescending look – he had no time for me! – and I left, angry and amazed at his short memory at my saving his bacon on The Manitou. Then, not too long after, as he was scouting locations for his next film, to be shot in the Philippines, his helicopter flew into a power line and he was killed. I was sent an invitation to the funeral by his widow, but, still angry and hurt at his arrogant dismissal of me, I couldn't bring myself to go to his funeral. I still have mixed feelings about it" – Thomas Pope.

21st Century Girdler

Today, many Girdler films are available as lavishly-packaged Blu Rays. A key element in this 21st century resurgence was the setting up of *William Girdler.com* in June 2000. The brainchild of self-confessed Girdler obsessive Patricia Breen, the site is a paradise for anyone seeking to know more, not only about Bill but also about regional and/or exploitation film-making in the 1970s. There's an awful lot of reading to be found there, especially given that the project was never finished. Not all of the films were examined in depth and some of the interviews trailed as forthcoming never materialized but one can find musical extracts and clips, some extremely detailed synopses, a collection of Girdler newspaper cuttings, interviews with some key personnel and even a diary of Breen's trip to Louisville. She spells out her motivations on the last page of the site:

I am often asked, "Why in God's name are you doing this?" The short answer is: pure obsession. The long answer is: I think Girdler's career was extraordinary and ultimately tragic. I loved his films when I was a kid; I love them as an adult. And I'd very much like to see this site generate some renewed interest in his work (Breen 2000-1).

On the first page, the introductory article *Girdler 101* ends on an appropriately poignant note:

Following his death, the J.B. Speed Art Museum in Louisville dedicated a film collection in honor of William Girdler. The collection that bears his name features cinematic luminaries such as Lillian Gish and D.W. Griffith. None of Girdler's own movies are included in the collection (Breen 2000-1).

There were no updates to the site after 2001, possibly due to ill health and Patty Mahon nee Breen reportedly died on Christmas morning 2019. The site is still up and it remains essential for Girdler-philes.

In 2017, to commemorate their release of *Grizzly* and *Day of the Animals*, Severin Films brought out an enamel pin bearing the likeness of the director. Previous pins celebrated such cult figures as Klaus Kinski, Edwige Fenech and Donald Pleasance.

Project:Kill, Grizzly and *The Zebra Killer* (under one of its many alternative titles, *Combat Cops*) have all been screened on 35mm at the New Beverly Cinema in Los Angeles, now under the ownership of the film director Quentin Tarantino. The print of *Cops* is reportedly from the director´s personal collection.

In 2021, Regal Records from New Jersey brought out a limited edition *Three on a Meathook* 45 containing the American Xpress songs from the film. Pressed in blood-red vinyl, the sleeve bears a short synopsis (which gives away the ending) and the message, ´In memory of William Girdler`

The director didn´t live to see John Frankenheimer´s *Prophecy* (1979), an eco-horror film about mercury leaking from a factory and creating a killer mutant bear. It´s plays like a rip-off of/homage to Girdler, what with the ecological warning of *Day of the Animals*, the Native American mythology of *The Manitou* and a *Grizzly*-style monster bear (although when we finally get a good look at *Prophecy*´s creature, it´s a far cry from the real animal in the earlier film). The director of *The Manchurian Candidate* (1962) and *Seconds* (1966) ripping off the King of the Knock-Offs!? I like to think Bill would have got a kick out of that.

Bibliography

Adams, D. (1977) "*The Manitou* film review". The Manitou 1977, directed by William Girdler | Film review (timeout.com)

Alexander, C. (2016) "Forget *The Exorcist*! Here's *Abby*!" Comingsoon.net

Albright, B. (2012) *Regional Horror Films, 1958–1990: A State-by-State Guide with Interviews*. Jefferson, North Carolina: McFarland and Company.

Anderson, J.M. (2007) "*The Manitou* review", Combustible Celluloid.com

anon a. (1977) "Crash kills Filmmaker William Girdler", *The Courier-Journal*. 01/23/1978.

anon b. (2014) "Cult Louisville Film Director Girdler's 1975 Flick 'Sheba Baby' Playing This Weekend", *Louisville Future*. https://louisvillefuture.com/archived-news/lou-cult-film-director-girdlers-sheba-baby-playing-weekend/

anon c. (1974) "Screen: '*Abby*', about a Black Family and Exorcism", *The New York Times*. 12/26/1974. Screen:' Abby,' About a Black Family and Exorcism - The New York Times (nytimes.com)

anon d. (1977) "Animals on the Rampage", *The New York Times*. 05/26/1977.

Aquino, M, (1983) *The Church of Satan*. San Francisco, California: CreateSpace Independent Publishing Platform.

Biodrowski, S (2007) "*Masque of the Red Death*, a retrospective", *Cinefantastique* Online. Masque of the Red Death (1964) – A Retrospective – Cinefantastique (cinefantastiqueonline.com)

Breen, Patricia (2000 -1) *William Girdler.com*

Brunson, M. (2019) "*The Manitou* review", Film Frenzy.

Buck, D (2017) "*Combat Cops*", Offscreen. Combat Cops (aka, The Zebra Killer, aka, The Get-Man, William Girdler, 1973) – Offscreen

Calvert, A. (1972) ""*Satan*" is just a devilishly awful movie", *The Voice-Jeffersonian*, 9/27/1972.

Canby, V. (1976) "William Girdler's Not-Quite-So-Toothsome 'Grizzly`, *The New York Times*.05/13/1977.

Clover, C. (1992) *Men, Women and Chainsaws: Gender in the Modern Horror Film.* Princeton University Press.

Cooper, I. (2016) *Frightmares: A History of British Horror.* Leyton Buzzard: Auteur Press.

Cooper, I. (2018) *The Manson Family on Film and Television.* Jefferson, North Carolina: McFarland and Company.

Culfilmalley (2020) "The Rip-Off Cult of William Girdler (Parts One and Two)", Cult Film Alley.

Dietrich, J. (undated) "Pam Grier interview", *The Courier-Journal.*

Ebert, R. (1973) "*Coffy* review". RogerEbert.com. https://www.rogerebert.com/reviews/coffy-1973

Ellis, L. (1971) "Horrors!", *The Courier-Journal.* 12/5/1971.

Ellroy, J. (1999) "Glamour Jungle", *Crime Wave.* London: Arrow Books. Pgs. 63-94.

Fine, M. (2005) *Bloody Sam: The Life and Times of Sam Peckinpah.* New York: Hyperion.

Flint, D. (2021) "The Eco-Horror Films of William Girdler", The Reprobate. The Eco-Horror Films Of William Girdler – The Reprobate (reprobatepress.com)

Frentzen, J. (1978) "William Girdler on *The Manitou*", *Cinefantastique* vol 06 no 4.

Fright, M. (2011) "He could've been a contender: The films of William Girdler", Mr. Frights's Scary Stuff. He could've been a contender: The films of William Girdler | Mr. Frights's Scary Stuff (wordpress.com)

Haberman, C. (2010) "Retrospective:1980's Slice of Sasquatchploitation *Night of the Demon*", Dread Central.com. Retrospective: 1980's Slice of Sasquatchploitation - Night of the Demon | Horror Movie, DVD, & Book Reviews, News, Interviews at Dread Central (archive.org)

Hammen, S. (1976) "Grizzly looks lot like shark", *The Courier-Journal.*

Harris, T. (2020) "Kentucky's Ed Wood: William Girdler and the Asylum of Satan", *Podcasting Them Softly.*

Hasan, M.R. (2017) Film: Abby, *KQEK.com.*

Heller-Nicholas, A. (2011) *Rape-Revenge Films: A Critical Study.* Jefferson, North Carolina: McFarland and Company.

Jones, D. & Moss, J. (2019) "Funning with the Devil", *Louisville Magazine.* September.

Kent, L. (1977) "Werner Herzog: 'Film Is Not the Art of Scholars, But of Illiterates'", *The New York Times.* 9/11/1977.

Kitley, J. (2016) "Interivew (sic.): Andrew Prine", Kitley's Krypt.

Klemesrud, J. (1974) "They Wait Hours to be Shocked", *The New York Times.* 01/24/1974.

Kohnhorst, M. (undated) Bio, *michael kohnhorst.com*

Knipfel, J. (2016) "William Girdler, King of the Knockoffs", *Den of Geek.* William Girdler, King of the Knockoffs - Den of Geek Knipfel

Knipfel, J. (2017) "When *Exorcist* Knockoffs Go Wrong: *The Manitou*", Den of Geek. When Exorcist Knockoffs Go Wrong: The Manitou | Den of Geek.

Lew, L. (2015) ""*Zebra Killer*" Who Inspired One Of The Most Racist Exploitation Films Ever Made Dies", The Underground Multiplex. https://theundergroundmultiplex.wordpress.com/2015/03/14/murderer-who-inspired-one-of-the-most-racist-exploitation-movies-ever-made-dies/

Long, J. (1971) "Devilish Doings, Cinematic satan stalks Louisville area; his motive is profit", *The Courier-Journal.* 11/22/1971.

Masterton, G. (1976) *The Manitou*. Pinnacle Books.

Masterton, G. (2014) "Horror Author Interviews", Ginger Nuts of Horror.

McDonagh, M. (2004) "Masters of Exploitation in Horwath", Alexander; Elsaesser, Thomas; King, Noel (eds.). *The Last Great American Picture Show: New Hollywood Cinema in the 1970s*. Amsterdam University Press. Pgs. 107-130.

Newman, K.(1988), *Nightmare Movies*. New York: Harmony Books.

Newman, K. (2022) "Film Review: *Abby*," The Kim Newman website. johnnyalucard.com

Nordern, E. (1968) "*Playboy* Interview: Stanley Kubrick", *Playboy* magazine. September 1968.

Padua, P. (2020) "Rediscover *Three on a Meathook*", Spectrum Culture. Rediscover: Three on a Meathook - Spectrum Culture

Palmer, R. (2000) *Herschell Gordon Lewis, Godfather of Gore: The Films*. Jefferson, North Carolina: McFarland & Company

Po, E. (2020) "How Hollywood Movie *Wonder Women* Was Shot In Manila", *Esquire.com*. Wonder Women Was Shot in Manila (esquiremag.ph)

Puchalski, S. (2000) *The Zebra Killer*, Shock Cinema. The Zebra Killer (shockcinemamagazine.com)

Rondinone, T. (2019) "Scary asylums are a Halloween classic, but it's time to retire the trope", *The Washington Post*. 10/31/2019. https://www.washingtonpost.com/outlook/2019/10/31/scary-asylums-are-halloween-classic-its-time-retire-trope/

Shand, J.P, Friedman, S.H. & Forsen, F.E. (2014) "The horror, the horror:stigma on screen", *The Lancet*. https://www.thelancet.com/journals/lanpsy/article/PIIS2215-0366(14)00014-5/fulltext

Veneman, J. (2002) "*Abby*'s Lazarus Soul: William Girdler's Tale of Demon Posession (sic.) in Search of a New Audience", *Monsterzine* #7.

Vorel, J. (2017) "From *Grizzly* to *Great White*: The Death of Film Ventures International", Paste. From Grizzly to Great White: The Death of Film Ventures International - Paste (pastemagazine.com)

Weber, B. (2010) "William Norton, Writer Wilder Than His Movies, Is Dead at 85", *The New York Times*. 10/8/2010.

Weldon, M.J. (1983) *The Psychotronic Encyclopaedia of Film*. London: Plexius.